THE
WIDOW
WORE
PINK

He is faithful
Robford

THE
WIDOW
WORE
PINK

A True Story of Life After Loss
and the Transforming Power
of a Loving God

ROBYN DYKSTRA

Gossamer Press

THE WIDOW WORE PINK:
A True Story of Life After Loss and the Transforming Power of a Loving God

Copyright © 2015 by Robyn Dykstra
Gossamer Press, LLC

978-0-9963681-0-0 Hardcover
978-0-9963681-1-7 Paperback
978-0-9963681-3-1 CD Audiobook
978-0-9963681-2-4 Ebook
978-0-9963681-4-8 Downloadable MP3

Editor: David Lambert
Cover design: Adazing Book Marketing
Interior design: Katherine Lloyd, The DESK

Printed in the United States of America

15 16 17 18 19 20 21 • 10 9 8 7 6 5 4 3 2 1

To my beautiful and brilliant mom.
For the courage you demonstrated,
and the choices you made possible for me.

To my personal muse, Amanda.
Were it not for her inspiration,
this manuscript would still be in my head,
and not in your hand.

To Dave, Mr. 4-Ever.
For your vision and tireless support.

To Jake & Eli.
Know that wherever you go and whatever you do,
there is a gossamer thread, spun airy thin with love,
from my heart to yours.

To Jesus.
I will always make your name known
and known better to those who need you
and need you more.

CONTENTS

Chapter 1

THE PLAYBOY CLUB

I stood half-naked in front of her desk trying to look more confident than I felt. I remained stock still, like a mannequin, in my high heels and leotard as she continued to scribble away on the application of the girl who had preceded me.

When she looked up, she smiled a small smile. An *it feels like you are the 10,000th girl in my office today and I'm tired* smile.

A *don't get your hopes up* smile.

"I am the Bunny Mother for this Playboy Club. If you are chosen to represent Playboy as a Bunny, I will be your supervisor."

I nodded slightly, still smiling my best Miss America imitation.

"Please turn around slowly," she said, picking up my application.

Three hundred sixty degrees later, she tilted her head slightly to the left and said, "Tell me your name."

"Robyn Leigh Landon."

"Well, Ms. Landon, what makes you think you'd be a good Playboy Bunny?"

"I'm smart and I'm pretty and I know how to make men smile," I blurted, with more exuberance than I intended.

Bunny Mother G smiled, apparently amused. "I'll make my decision by the end of the week. You'll be notified by telephone if you're selected. Thank you for coming in today."

She began scribbling on my application. I was dismissed.

I stepped out of her office and back into the Bunnies' dressing room, where I checked my reflection in the full-length mirror. At five eight and 125 pounds, I had no bosom to speak of. But on the plus side, as ungainly and ordinary as I had been as a youngster, by high school I had blossomed into a beauty—tall and thin, with long auburn hair and longer legs that were voted "the best of" in my class. Everything on me was matched and symmetrical. I had never had acne or a weight problem. But here, clothed in a leotard left over from a high-school gymnastics class, surrounded by stunning women, I felt small and out of place, like when you show up at a party in jeans and everyone else is in an evening gown.

I drove home discouraged about the interview, comparing myself to both all the other beauties auditioning and those already employed, certain that I would never get the callback. I dreaded my future. My two options: return to college in the fall, which didn't appeal to me at all, or continue to work as a bank teller, wearing a brown polyester uniform five days a week and making almost enough money to pay for my car insurance, rent, and partying.

I'd spotted Playboy's help-wanted ad for Bunnies in the Sunday newspaper two weeks earlier. Open interviews were being held at the Lake Geneva Playboy Club, only seventy miles from my home in Madison, Wisconsin, on a Saturday morning, which wouldn't interfere with my lousy job at the bank. Applicants were to bring a swimsuit or leotard and valid ID to prove they were at least eighteen—old enough to serve liquor. No résumé or previous experience necessary. Was that suspicious?

Screwing up my courage, I'd carried the newspaper ad into the living room where my mom was reading. I sat on the couch next to her and showed her the ad. "What do you think of this?" I asked. Bear in mind that my mom is seriously smart and serious about women's rights. She got her PhD in Educational Administration with an emphasis on Affirmative Action for Women. I was prepared for a lecture on the subjugation of women or Playboy's degradation of women. Maybe even some expletives about a company that exalted male chauvinism.

Mom had pushed hard for me to attend college, hoping, I'm sure, that

I would catch her obsession for academic learning, something I had not inherited. And I'm sure she considered it an added benefit that I would be far removed from my hot-headed, alcoholic ex-boyfriend. After one dismal year of college experience, I announced that I was done! "I'm not going back. It's hard. Why do I need to go to college now? I don't know what I want to BE! I hate school and I hate being broke all the time!"

When I dropped out, she said, "If you aren't going back to college, you'll have to get a job, pay rent, take care of your own insurance and car. I'm happy to provide those things for you if you're a student, but you can handle them now."

Smart, my mom. She knew I wasn't qualified to work at anything that would support me in the manner to which I was accustomed. She gambled that if she let *me* figure that out, I'd be happy to go back to college.

After working as a bank teller for months, being forced to wear the ugliest uniform ever and making practically nothing, I was eager to find something else. Hence, the perusal of the help-wanted ads.

"Maybe I could just work there for the summer—you know, make some good money, then go back to school," I said as she stared at the newspaper.

When she finished reading, she looked up and said, "Go for it."

What?

"You can always go to school," she continued. "I'm sure the window for being a Playboy Bunny doesn't stay open very long. You'd be great at it! When is the interview?"

I was flabbergasted. There wasn't a trace of sarcasm in her voice—she was genuine and encouraging. Who *was* this woman? The mother who raised me had marched at women's rights rallies where other women burned their bras. (My practical mother never parted with her Playtex 18-Hour Comfort Strap bra out of necessity. Her full-figured bazooms needed the support. All the women on my mom's side had been full-figured. My grandma used to shake her head and cluck to herself about my itty-bitties. "Well, maybe they'll grow when you have babies." Mom had said dryly, "Big breasts are a pain. She's better off without them. They just attract the wrong kind of man.")

"Really, you think it's okay?" I stammered, still waiting for the ax to fall.

She, who had INSISTED that I go to college to avoid any chance of working at this type of job said, "Sure. Go see what they say."

With her surprising approval, I drove to the interview not entirely certain what being a Playboy Bunny even meant. I didn't know anyone who had been a Bunny. Of course, I had seen the magazines, which occasionally found their way into our house—my mom actually read the articles. We didn't think of them as pornography. According to the First Amendment and my mother, *Playboy* had just as much right to publish as *Time* or *Life* or *Psychology Today*.

The ad hadn't been very specific about the job description. And since my slightly rusted '68 Camaro SS had no radio, my mind had plenty of silence to speculate about being a Bunny. I'd never worked in a restaurant—would someone teach me what to do? Was "cocktail service" code for something else? Would it be safe to work there? Would I make lots of money? Would there be a hidden subculture of prostitution? Would I be expected to have sex with someone to get the job? And if so—would I?

I had been sexually active for years. Like so many of us in the '70s, I believed my body was mine to do with as I pleased. I believed there was such a thing as safe sex, and that if I was responsible, my choice to have sex wouldn't hurt me or anyone else. For me, sex was an extremely effective tool of manipulation. Men were so ridiculously willing to do or say anything to see a naked woman. I had sex for fun, for favors, and for sympathy. For birthday presents and parting gifts. I used sex to keep from having uncomfortable conversations and to say I'm sorry. I thought sex was part and parcel of life—not just as a Bunny, but as a woman.

I got a high from sexual skirmishes, but I longed to have a more substantive relationship. I knew I wasn't designed to be alone. I wanted to be treasured inside a monogamous relationship, but I settled for being tantalizing. Sex provided me an "adoration fix." I thought that eventually I would fall into bed with Mr. Right who would love me, marry me, and cherish me forever because the sex was good. Maybe Mr. Right was waiting for me at the Playboy Club.

A guard at the front entrance greeted me politely, then opened the gate to a long, winding driveway. I drove past landscaped acres of flowers and sculpted bushes, past ponds and golf-course green as far as I could see. At the 350-room, Frank Lloyd Wright–inspired hotel, smartly uniformed bellhops directed me and a horde of other applicants through a gorgeous lobby and down artfully decorated hallways to the office of the Bunny Mother.

The luxury abruptly ended at the doorway that divided the guest areas from the employee section of the hotel. The Bunnies' locker room and Bunny Mother's office were in the basement. I passed the small glass-faced offices of the Bunny Mother and her assistant on my way to the dressing room, where the dreary starkness disappointed me. I'd expected a swanky suite of dressing rooms. There was nothing pretty or even feminine about this room—it was smoky and dingy, with walls of pale yellow cinder block. Rows of gray lockers lined the walls, and another island of them stood off-center in the dressing room. Along the farthest wall, twenty feet of mirrors hung above a long counter, under which sat ten or twelve chairs. Off to the right were more lockers and a shower area. Off to the left was the seamstress's room, where the costumes were hung.

The message was clear: Bunnies were not divas. They were interchangeable cogs, like table settings or golf carts.

I was given a brief application to complete and told to change into my swimsuit or leotard. "Everyone will get a personal interview with the Bunny Mother," said her assistant. We changed our clothes in the open area between the mirrored vanity and the lockers. Uncomfortable, I looked for a spot that afforded some cover; I saw many others doing the same. It was like the first gym class in junior high. Awful! We sat or stood awkwardly, watching perfectly coiffed Bunnies enter and exit for their shifts. There were no modesty issues for them. *Keep your mouth closed and don't stare!* I told myself. I was used to being the pretty one in every room, but here, everyone was arm candy!

Two days after the interview, I got the call: "You're hired. Report for training in ten days."

I moved into the Bunny Dorm with some of the other newbies. A single-story barracks surrounded by cyclone fencing, it sat at the edge of one of the golf courses. There were two wings of bedrooms furnished with bunk beds and dressers for double occupancy, joined in the center by a living room common area. Bunnies with some seniority had their own rooms; others shared a room. Sometimes there were forty Bunnies living there. My roommate didn't make it through the first week of training, so I ended up with a room to myself.

The Bunny Dorm was surprisingly quiet, considering that it was always filled with girls in various stages of drama. During off-duty hours, it was a place for us to watch soap operas and talk about boyfriends, about home, how much our feet hurt, which busboys were best to work with, our schedules—and always, how much money we made.

If visitors had been allowed in, we would have been hard-pressed to convince them we were the same glamour girls who had just waited on them. We ran around in ratty, loose-fitting clothes, our faces often smudged with makeup from the previous shift, our hair wadded up in ponytails. There was a sorority feel to it, without the stress of exams. After training week, that is.

All new Bunnies went through seven days of instruction with a trainer in a classroom, then seven days following an experienced Bunny on the floor. I worked for restaurant worker's minimum wage—$2.20 an hour with no tips until I was allowed to work solo.

The first day, I was fitted for my uniform. New Bunnies got two reconditioned costumes. I got a bright yellow one and a zigzagged printed one. After you'd been there for a while, Playboy seamstresses made costumes specifically for you. Black was the most coveted color and hardest to get at our Club. The bodice of the costume was strapless and fully padded at the bosom with metal stays the length of the corset to mold the body's form. For girls like me who missed the big breast gene, the seamstress showed us how to stuff padding into the cups to create fullness, even cleavage! Hurrah! Turned out, *most* Bunnies needed the extra stuffing in their costumes.

Three pairs of eyelets high on the French-cut leg were threaded with laces and tied in a bow on which pens, tiny flashlights, and wine openers were hung.

Pressed and starched collars and cuffs sat in piles in a box in the costume room. To the collar we added a black bowtie, and to the white cuffs, Playboy cufflinks. "Make sure your cufflinks are kissing," instructed Bunny Alison, getting ready for her shift. "See how the Playboy heads face each other when you put your wrists together? You don't want to get a demerit for facing them away from each other."

Helga, the seamstress, handed me a headband with a pair of Bunny ears covered with the same fabric as my costume. I secured them to my head with bobby pins. "You bend zem like zis," Helga said in her strong Polish accent, demonstrating. We were allowed to shape the ears to reflect our personality, but too insecure to be playful or suggestive with them, I left them just the way they were. *If that's how the Bunny before me wore them, then that's fine with me,* I thought. I just wanted to blend in until I could get the lay of the land.

To prevent jiggling, we all wore nude support hose under sheer black pantyhose, the cost of which was deducted from our paychecks.

The last thing Helga handed me was my tail. "Brush it to keep it fluffy," she said as she attached it to my backside on the three hooks and eyes that kept it in place. She gave it a pat. "Now, look at me, and stand up straight," she told us all. There was nothing see-through about the Bunny costume, and yet it created an alluring and sexy look to the patrons. We all posed in front of the mirrors, turning this way and that to catch every angle of our transformed bodies. We all had colorful hourglass figures; our padded bosoms nearly spilling out of the cups of our costumes. The black hose and high-heeled pumps made even the shortest girls look leggy.

The final accessory to be attached to the costume was the name tag—a three-inch rosette that looked like the award ribbons at the county fair with a name badge in the center that hooked onto the left hip of my costume. "Vut iz your Bunny name?" asked Helga.

"Robyn," I replied.

"No!" she said, shaking her head. "There is already Robin, so you must choose another name. No duplicates!"

"Well, I don't know," I said, poking my finger into the box of black circles with white names. "How about Leigh? That's my middle name."

"No, already a Lee." She didn't shake her head this time. She was running out of patience with me. How many times had she gone through this? Just pick one!

I kept sifting the black badges. Nancy? Camilla? Amber? Pert? Nothing seemed to fit. "How about Corey? Is there already a Corey?" I asked, picking a badge out of the box.

"No. No Corey. You be Corey. You look like Corey!"

"Whatever that means. Okay, I'll be Corey," I said disappointedly.

I fastened the Corey badge onto the black rosette. Helga hung it on my costume. "Okay, you ready? Good, you go now. Next!"

Once the twelve of us were suited up, we each stepped on the scale in the Assistant Bunny Mother's office and fiddled with the markers on the calibrated slide until the needle balanced in the middle, then called out the number to be written down.

Next was a tour of the main building. The confidence I felt in the locker room disintegrated as Bunny Mother G led us around as a mama duck leads her ducklings. We paraded through the building, attracting lots of attention. It wasn't rare to see Bunnies walking around the property, but it was rare to see so many of us in a bunch. "They must be new Bunnies," I heard guests say, pointing us out to each other as we passed through the halls. "How many will make it a month?" one seasoned Bunny asked in a stage whisper. Two of the girls in our troupe must have been in heels for the first time in their lives, because they scuffled along in their shoes, dragging their heels along. Other new Bunnies stared at the floor as if searching for land mines. A couple of the girls slumped, rolling their shoulders in, uncomfortable with their height or their newfound cleavage. Yes, we were quite a sight.

There were dozens of Playboy Clubs around the world in 1977, but the Club in Lake Geneva was a premier location, serving also as a hotel and resort. It sat on 1,400 lush and rolling acres; it had a landing strip for private planes and small jets and a stable for horses. We hosted activities for every season. There were two eighteen-hole golf courses designed by someone famous—probably a friend of Hef's. There were indoor and outdoor pools, a ski chalet featuring several ski slopes with chairlifts, five full-service restaurants, a showroom, and of course, a discotheque. The five restaurants on the property, not including the ProShop and Ski Chalet, varied in degrees of formality. I paid close attention to Bunny Mother G's narrative as we toured, because these restaurants would be where I made my money. The finer the restaurant experience, the heftier the price, and the bigger potential for tips for me.

"All new Bunnies start in the Sidewalk Café," she said over her shoulder, "a sandwich shop serving gourmet burgers and quick meals." She gestured with one hand, her high heels clicking on the pebbled floor. She didn't look down or scuffle. She walked like she'd been born in high heels. We clicked along behind her, people continuing to stare at the gaggle of us.

Across the hall was another restaurant. "The Living Room is a buffet," Bunny Mother G said without slowing down, gesturing with her other hand. "New Bunnies sometimes work in the Living Room, depending on the hotel occupancy." Meaning that if the hotel was so full that Bunnies with seniority were needed elsewhere, spots in the Living Room would go to newer Bunnies. "Guests get their own food, and Bunnies provide cocktail service for lunch and dinner. Waitresses work the breakfast shift. No one expects to see a glamorous Bunny in the early morning." I sighed with relief when I saw the hours of operation on the sign in front of the buffet—it opened at 7:00 a.m.

Farther down the hallway was the Bunny Hutch, a discotheque. "You serve cocktails, and you may dance with customers." She stopped, turned, and looked straight at us. "You may not slow dance or allow a guest to touch you." Then she pivoted and led on.

At the end of the hall, past the souvenir counter, was the Playboy Club dining room. The rest of the facility was open to the public, but the Playboy Club dining room was for members only. Key cards could be purchased by mail or at the gift shop for $25.00 a year. Silver cards were entrance-only cards; guests settled their bill in cash or with a credit card or room charge. Gold cards were charge cards, with virtually no limit on the property. Gold VIP cards were issued almost exclusively to personal friends of Hugh Hefner, so the very best of service was expected and only exemplary Bunnies were assigned to serve those guests.

The Playboy Club dining room was the hotel's fine dining experience, featuring two adjoining, split-level rooms for food service and a cocktail area and bar called the Playmate Lounge. It came by that name because the wall behind the bar, from one end to the other, was a collage of—you guessed it—Playmates, centerfolds from the magazine in all their naked perfection, thanks to wonderful genetics and airbrushing.

Bunnies were rarely centerfolds.

A French restaurant called the VIP Room and the Cabaret, a Las Vegas-type showroom where Bunnies worked in teams with waiters, were on the second floor. New Bunnies did not get to work those rooms. However, since the Cabaret was open only at night, it could be used for training during the day, and the Bunny Mother led us there next. Using the Bunny Handbook as a syllabus and demonstrating Bunny Stance for us as she talked, Bunny Mother G reviewed her expectations of us. Bunny Stance is like third position in ballet.

"Bunnies must *always* maintain Bunny Image," she began.

"Bunnies must be beautiful and fresh looking. Failure to meet and maintain Playboy's standard of Bunny Image will result in dismissal.

"Bunnies wear vivid, bright lipstick at all times.

"Bunnies must have manicured nails, coated with a non-translucent polish at all times.

"Bunnies wear false eyelashes for every shift, even if you are working poolside or on the golf course.

"Bunnies are hired with a certain look. Changing your hair color or style in a way that is no longer considered Bunny Image is cause for suspension or dismissal.

"Bunnies weigh in every Saturday without exception. Changes to your weight that affect your Bunny Image are cause for suspension or dismissal.

"Bunnies do not eat, drink, smoke, or sit in front of customers.

"Bunnies do not sit; they perch, legs crossed at the ankles." She demonstrated.

"Bunnies are not allowed to eat at the restaurants alone. You must have another Bunny with you at all times.

the meals, cleaned up everything, and earned 20 to 25 percent of the tips, depending on the service, the Bunny's mood, and the take. I had very few shifts in the Bunny Hutch or Sidewalk Café after that.

Bunnies were expected to do special promotions for the Playboy Club. I played basketball and softball for charity events. Team Bunny always won, not because we were so good but because it was just part of the deal. We wore bright lipstick and false eyelashes and did our hair for every game. Lots of companies had their sales meetings and golf outings on the property and would hire Bunnies to drive golf carts and serve beverages, wearing short shorts and tight T-shirts with the Playboy logo strategically placed across our chests.

I was featured in the Best Bunnies section of *Playboy* magazine two of the years I was at Playboy and was a Bunny spokesperson for the Lake Geneva Playboy Club for television news pieces and newspaper articles. I was featured in two television pieces on entertainment shows, one shown nationally. I was a natural for the job of Training Bunny. For three years, I was the one demonstrating the Bunny Dip to gawking new Bunnies.

My tips were a tangible measure of success or failure. I worked hard to make sure my guests got great service and bragging rights about their visit to my Playboy Club. I considered the tips I earned an entitlement. I ran all my stations with precision. I had high expectations of the boys assigned to me and tipped them accordingly, so we both made money. Every shift I put on that Bunny costume was a new competition to see if I could best my previous high score. The men, the guests in my station, were unknowing players in my game. If they got good service and tipped well, everybody won.

I loved being a Bunny. That summer job lasted four years.

"If you come back to the Club to eat, you are never to sit at any bar, alone or attended. It's tacky.

"Bunnies are not allowed to date customers. Dating customers is cause for dismissal.

"Bunnies are not allowed in any of the hotel rooms for any reason. Any Bunny discovered in any part of the hotel will be dismissed.

"Bunnies may not be in the company of any male on the property without a permission slip from me, which must be obtained twenty-four hours in advance. That applies to male relatives. Bunnies on the property with a male without proper permission will be dismissed.

"Bunnies who miss a shift because of sickness must bring in a doctor's note to return to work. Failure to provide a doctor's note is cause for dismissal."

Playboy wanted Bunnies to be walking fantasies and Playboy's walking fantasies were not to be associated with other organizations. Or be nearsighted. Or married. Therefore, according to the Bunny Handbook, we did not have tattoos, wear eyeglasses, or wear jewelry of any kind except for the regulation Playboy cufflinks we were issued. No earrings, no wedding rings.

Bunny Mother G talked for nearly two hours. "Now, let's have a look at all of you," she said finally, wrapping up. We all rose and stood in Bunny Stance. She slowly walked the line, making suggestions:

"You need darker lipstick.

"You'll have to wear a darker nail color. Lighter colors don't work well.

"Stop biting your nails—it's a horrible habit.

"I'd like to see some bangs.

"Where are your shoes?" she asked me. Somehow I'd missed the memo about what kind of shoes I would need. The cute, strappy sandals I'd brought didn't cut it. Playboy required plain, closed-toe pumps—no straps, no decorations, dyed or painted to match the costume with a minimum heel height of three inches. "You can wear those today," Bunny Mother G said, "but you will need Bunny shoes by tomorrow."

When the inspection was finished, she resumed her Bunny Stance actresses or centerfolds or were there to hook a sugar daddy, but most of us were just working a job that paid well while we waited for Mr. Right, or saved for college, or decided what to do with the rest of our lives. None of us thought we would be collecting retirement checks from Playboy— we all knew it was a seasonal job, and that season lasted exactly as long as your Bunny Image.

Bunnies who were hired in at approximately the same time tended to clique up. We had shared training experiences, usually worked similar shifts, and made about the same kind of money. Some of the Bunnies had been there for five years or more when I was hired. A few had been there when the Club was new and exclusive. When it had attracted executive types with fat paychecks and expensive tastes. When the Playboy Bunny was considered more risqué than adorable. Those Bunnies had been there when it rained money, and they knew all the tricks of making big tips. They were single and smart; they had invested their money in real estate and stocks. They carried Louis Vuitton bags, used Estee Lauder department-store makeup, wore fur coats, and had their jeans dry-cleaned. They drove Porsches and Corvettes to work. I used Maybelline and shopped at J.C. Penney.

Still, what a great gig! Bunnies never carried big trays; male food runners and busboys carried them for us. My food runner would bring out a tray of entrées and a jack stand to set the tray on and place it next to a table in my station. He would pull the silver cover off the entrée so I could lift the plate off the tray and set it in front of my guest, then he'd whisk away the tray and silver food covers. When guests left, a busboy would clean it all up for the next group. For all that, they earned about 15 to 20 percent of a Bunny's take for the shift.

When I was trained for the Cabaret Showroom, it became my favorite shift. I was soon making in a couple of nights what it would have taken me all month to make at any other legal summer job. Everyone streamed in simultaneously, ate dinner, watched the show, tipped well, and left en masse. Bunnies were paired with a single food runner/busboy who did most of the work. We took the drink orders, provided ambiance, and collected the money. The young men took the dinner orders, delivered

Chapter 2

FAIRY TALES

hardly see you anymore," I whispered to Marshall, snuggled up next to him with my head on his bare shoulder. "I miss you."

"You work weekends and random nights. I work during the week. Our schedules don't go together like they used to."

"You could visit me more often at the Club."

"There's no place to stay. You can't be in the hotel rooms and I can't come to your room at the dorm. Hotel rooms in Lake Geneva cost too much even when they are available."

I sat up and lit a cigarette. It was tough to maintain relationships as a Bunny, and adding the complication of long distance to ours wasn't helping.

Marshall propped himself on one elbow so he could look at me. "You could move in with me."

It was the proposal I'd been waiting for. Or so I thought.

Marshall and I had met the spring of my first and only year away at college. Another coed, Maura, had pleaded, "Come out with me this weekend. I can hook you up with some cute guys from my hometown. Aren't you tired of frat boys and jocks?"

We hitchhiked the ten miles to her hometown bar, and it was bustling. Maura introduced me around, and there really were lots of cute guys, but there was instant chemistry between Marshall and me. He sat at the end of the bar drinking Bacardi and Coke. Drink in one hand, cigar in the other, gorgeous. He looked like he belonged on a billboard selling cigarettes, or beer, or underwear. He had black, shoulder-length, wavy hair, a thick black mustache, and dark blue eyes. I watched him shake bar dice for rounds of drinks or a pile of dollar bills. Players take turns shaking the dice in a leather cup, then slam it upside down on the bar. The sequence of the dice determines who continues to play and who ends up paying for the round or wins the pot of bills. As a college student, I didn't have any money to play, but Marshall and I played as a team—he paid and I shook the dice. We won round after round. "Shake 'em again, darlin'. I think you're lucky!" he'd say. As the bar filled up, the space between us closed until I was pressed between his legs, my hip in his crotch. His hand slipped around my waist and rested on my belly.

I had never been much of a drinker. Just one dismally embarrassing experience in high school with malt liquor had cured me. I'd been sixteen and hanging out with a gang of guys who dressed like motorcyclists from the '50s: leather jackets, greased-back hair, the whole getup. We'd listen to oldies and go to dances to twist and jitterbug. Mostly, we just walked around town or sat in the park talking and smoking. One night, the boys showed up with cute little cans of Schlitz Malt Liquor. "Way classier than beer," they told me.

I took one taste and said, "This is horrible. It tastes like horse pee smells. I can't drink this!"

Their solution? "Chug it!"

I managed to get down one can before I started vomiting. I couldn't stop. I kept puking so violently that they called my mother, who came to get me. To her supreme satisfaction, I was nauseated for three days.

Wedged next to Marshall, I spent the night shaking bar dice and drinking my Coca-Cola. I danced a couple of songs with Maura. After a couple of hours, she disappeared, but I didn't care. I was having a great time with Marshall.

At closing time he asked, "How about I give you a ride home since it looks like your friend left with my brother?"

I never thought twice about the fact that he'd been drinking all night. We walked out to the parking lot and he stopped at a white Corvette.

"No way! This is your car?" I asked.

"Yes it is, young lady. Get in!"

I lowered myself into the car and he shut my door. "This is so cool. I have a Camaro SS at home in storage," I said.

"Let me know if you ever want to sell it. I wheel and deal cars."

Marshall drove me back to my dorm. "How 'bout you give me your number? We could go out again." I gave it to him. He called the next day. And the next. And the next.

A pleasant routine developed. Every Friday night, he'd vroom up to my dorm in whatever spiffy sports car or schmooze-mobile he had that week and we'd spend the weekend together. He would take me to a supper club for dinner: Fridays were fish-fry nights and Saturday was prime rib. We'd spend most of our weekend nights in one tavern or another, playing bar dice, Marshall drinking his rum and Cokes till last call. Then we'd get food at a truck stop or diner, either with friends or alone, and get a hotel room. During the day we'd go look at cars he thought he might buy or meet someone who was interested in buying a car from him. Sunday afternoon, he'd return me to my dorm.

When the school year ended, I moved back home to Madison and took the teller job at the bank. As he had for many summers, Marshall moved to Illinois where he worked as an iron worker. He stayed in Illinois till the bitter winter weather prohibited climbing around on the skeletons of tall buildings high above the ground. In winter, he migrated back to Wisconsin, collected unemployment checks, and flipped used cars.

Our routine didn't change; we just traveled longer distances. I'd drive to Illinois on Wednesday after work and spend the night with him at his place. He'd take me out for an Italian dinner and I'd say thank you with sex. Thursday morning, I'd get up super early to drive the sixty-five miles back to Madison for work. On weekends, Marshall would stay with me at Mom's house in Madison. Mom didn't mind that we stayed together at her house. It was sensible and responsible. Some nights her boyfriend would stay too. We were very civilized.

My mother loved me to the moon and back, but her parenting had always been unconventional. My parents divorced when I was three. Divorce was not the norm in 1959, and in Wisconsin a divorce wasn't granted unless someone had been very naughty. That wasn't the case with my folks; they just outgrew each other. They had started out with the common denominators: They were high-school sweethearts who shared their peers, their community, and their interest in making my dad happy. Mom was the student. Dad was the athlete, required to maintain a certain GPA to participate in sports. They studied together until Dad had to run off to a practice or a game, then Mom would finish both his homework and her own.

After my dad graduated, he followed his brothers into the armed forces, serving in the navy while Mom finished three more years of high school. She said her senior year was a breeze, since she had completed the coursework once before. She graduated as class valedictorian.

Dad got home from Korea just as Mom started her first term at the University of Wisconsin. On September 12, 1954, Mama's nineteenth birthday, they eloped to the Little Brown Church near Waterloo, Iowa. They got married, got a hotel room to consummate the proceedings, then went right back to their parents' houses, where they kept their little secret for several weeks.

Of course, when they announced the news, everyone assumed Mom was pregnant. She wasn't, or else she had the longest pregnancy in history since I wasn't born until two years later. Although she was technically a virgin when they got married, she admits that they'd been at the precipice of intercourse many times before their honeymoon. After all the anticipation and everything-but-intercourse sex, she said her wedding night was the worst sex of her life. Couldn't figure out what all the fuss about. Later, she wondered whether, if she had slept with my dad before the wedding, they ever would have gotten married. She wondered whether all the pressure to stay pure forced her to marry someone she just wanted to have sex with, not spend the rest of her life with.

There's no doubt that they loved each other, but the ground they shared quickly shrank until there was only enough room for one, and my mother left him to occupy it. After the divorce, I saw my dad only for birthdays and on Christmas. What I remember of him is gleaned largely from photographs of his infrequent visits.

Mom was given full custody, and we all—my younger brother included—moved in with her parents. As a single mom, she worked full-time, went to school full-time, and parented full-time. She completed her teaching certification and moved us to Portage, Wisconsin, to take a job as a high-school English teacher. She hired a nanny with whom she evenly split her paycheck, which seemed fair since they parented us as a team. Hum, as we called our sweet surrogate parent, was fragile-thin; her body, her hair, even her voice was thin. She didn't drive. We took lots of walks. She took thousands of pictures and mounted them on black pages of photo albums, meticulously labeling each one with the occasion and the date. She must have licked a billion black photo corners in the process.

Mom believed television rotted your brain, so she took the cord to our eight-inch, black-and-white TV set to work with her to prevent unauthorized viewing. I could read way before I went to kindergarten, and I had a college-level vocabulary in eighth grade.

We were broke but didn't know it. We had a little apartment and a big, black, Chevy four-door sedan from the '40s that had to warm up even if it was one hundred degrees outside; Mom named it Gertruda. We couldn't afford to feed a cat or dog, so Mom named inanimate objects to make them seem like family pets.

Mom met a fella she liked a lot and moved us to Waukegan, Illinois, to be closer to him. He taught music, choir, and band; she got a job at the same high school, teaching English.

We lived in a rented two-bedroom house a block away from our school. My brother, Dion, and I each got our own rooms. Mom walled off a tiny front part of the living room for her bed. She covered the wall with randomly sized rectangles that she painted in orange, green, and brown tones. The entry door to her room just looked like one of the other rectangles on the wall. Our house was the coolest. The other kids in the neighborhood always wanted to see the secret room with the hidden door.

In 1964, being divorced carried a stigma. Some families told their children not to play with us because they feared our bad influence as products of divorce. As if divorce was contagious. Dion and I were generally good kids but not immune to the gossip. One summer, bored and hopped up on Mountain Dew, we mischievously tore down flyers for a neighborhood carnival that we weren't invited to attend. The police actually came to the door and scared the fiendishness out of us with the threat of juvenile detention for vandalism. Mom lied through her teeth, saying we had been home with her and couldn't possibly have been the culprits. When I heard her committing perjury for us, I had a chilling realization of how easy it would be for the authorities to label Mom an unfit parent and remove my brother and me from her house.

Mom gave in to a second marriage, I believe, largely to protect us against criticism. She eloped with John Landon, the music teacher at the high school, and they filed for a quick adoption. Mr. Landon was a prime candidate for the Vietnam draft and eager to avoid it. As a married man with children, he was exempt. And my mom was keen on creating the illusion of a nuclear family.

My birth father had married Pat, wife number two, and they produced my half-sister, Paula. It was probably convenient for my dad to yield his parental rights so that Mr. Landon could adopt Dion and me, and I hope his decision was made, at least in part, to give everyone a fresh start.

The new Landon family moved into a two-story brick house on the corner lot of a nice neighborhood where couples wandered into each other's yards for beers and cookouts and their kids tore around on stingray bikes with banana seats and played kick the can until the porch lights came on and everyone was called home.

I am sure being married to my mom was an eye-opener for Mr. Landon, whose parents were very traditional. His mom had been at home full-time, taking care of the children, the house, the husband, and volunteering for women's clubs. What he had thought exhilarating and refreshingly different about my mom in the beginning were the same things that vexed and confounded him in the end. The marriage lasted less than a year. The week after fourth grade ended, as I packed to spend the summer (as usual) in the small town of Lodi, Wisconsin, with Grandma and Grandpa Clark, my mom packed her personal things too. We didn't go back to the brick house on the corner lot. We stayed a year at Grandma and Grandpa Clark's while Mom wrapped up a master's in English Literature and I rocked the fifth grade. I never saw Mr. Landon again.

When I was about thirteen, I found out why. I was rummaging through the sewing box to put a button back on Mom's blouse and found four slides of her with bruises down both arms and a swollen face. "Mom," I gasped, "When were these taken?" She looked at them and a sad smile crossed her lips. "They were taken as evidence for the divorce proceedings in Illinois. I wanted to make the judge was aware of our situation so that you and Dion would never be subjected to the kind of treatment I was." Since Mr. Landon had adopted Dion and me, there was a chance he could be granted visitation or even custody. Taking those pictures sealed the deal, despite the adoption.

When I was fifteen, she announced that either she had done a good job of teaching responsibility and instilling values or it was too late, and since she traveled so much for her job licensing high schools for the State of Wisconsin, and couldn't chain me to my bed, all my decisions and their consequences were now mine to manage and bear. She would not be bailing me out of jail, paying for abortions, or even signing excuse notes for missed days at school.

She also believed that all teens, including hers, would experiment with drugs, alcohol, and sex. So when I was fifteen and had my first steady boyfriend, she marched me to the gynecologist for birth control pills so I could have the benefit of safe sex. She wasn't as concerned about whether I was smoking pot as she was about where I did it, so she gave me permission to do drugs at home where it was safer. The legal drinking age was eighteen, which I turned the fall of my senior year. "Don't drink if you drive my car," was about all she said about it. I never had a curfew at her house, but regardless of nocturnal activities, I was expected to get to school on time, do the assignments, and get myself to work.

At sixteen, I got a job at the mall selling accessories like gloves, scarves, and purses. Mom showed me how to budget money. I was to buy all my own clothes and personal items and gasoline for the car and pay for my own entertainment. For the first few months, she sat down with graph paper and calculator to help me distribute the money I earned.

She got her PhD the year I graduated from high school. We both got class rings in 1975.

⸎

When Marshall began staying overnight with me at Mom's house, she had been dating Boyd for about a year. They were as serious as Mom was willing to get in a relationship; she had no desire to get married again. Their relationship was exclusive. They enjoyed lively conversations, were supportive of each other's career, and satisfied each other's needs for companionship.

Boyd wasn't really in Mom's league when they began dating. She was snazzy and classy. She contended in a man's world for equal pay and equal rights, yet she maintained her femininity. She wore dresses, curled her hair, put on lipstick to go out of the house, wore trendy jewelry, and smelled like perfume.

Boyd had a PhD like Mom but was more hippy-ish, more earthy. Even so, he was so stinkin' smart and like-minded that she couldn't help but adore him. When he first started coming around, his idea of dressing up was corduroy pants and a wool plaid shirt. He looked disheveled even on the rare occasions he wore a suit and tie. Mom taught him the value of a good haircut, a pressed shirt, and polished shoes. He even started wearing a dress coat and hat regularly. They each had their financial and professional independence, with all the benefits of a committed partnership. In all honesty, their relationship suited Mom better than Boyd. Eight years Mom's junior, I think he wanted to get married, maybe even have a couple of kids. Mom had been there and done that, and there was no way she was starting over.

Boyd and Marshall got along great. They talked about sports, politics, movies, and cars. They joked about the idiosyncrasies of their Landon women. Mom and I had the same laugh, used the same colloquialisms, and had the same obsession for cleanliness.

Mom liked Marshall but thought he was too much like my dad. Big football star from a small town, hungry for fancy cars and clothes at the expense of relationships.

I'd been living in the Bunny Dorm for about eight months when Marshall suggested cohabitation, which I assumed would naturally lead to a wedding. I thought we were on our way to happily-ever-after. Turns out, it was a proposal of convenience, not marriage.

"Can you bring home the Bunny outfit?" Marshall asked.

I rolled my eyes at him. "Nope, sorry. Taking a costume off the property is cause for dismissal."

Actually, I wasn't sorry at all. I thought it was a stupid idea. *That costume is nearly impenetrable, with all the stays and fittings. How sexy does he think it will be when I drop the stuffing from the cups onto the floor, then peel off two layers of pantyhose only to reveal skin covered with marks and indentations from the tight-fitting pieces? It's better in fantasy than in reality.*

Marshall wasn't ready for or interested in the kind of forever life I was dreaming of, in which we would build a home, family, and life together.

Marshall liked his money, and he didn't want to be saddled with the responsibility of a wife. He was the oldest of a passel of kids who had grown up in rural poverty on a big farm not far from Whitewater, Wisconsin, where I attended college. Later, his family had become prosperous, but by that time Marshall had left the farm so he could have the things his parents had not been able to provide. He still wanted to go where he wanted, to buy what he wanted, and to be with whomever he wanted. And to be fair, he had never promised me a wedding. When I talked about the future, he let me daydream. He didn't lie; he just didn't correct me. I saw living together as the pathway to the altar. He viewed living together as the best he could offer in terms of commitment. He bought the furniture, pots and pans, and a spice rack. We picked out bedding and towels and hung draperies in our little white house. We got a cat. I grocery shopped and he mowed the lawn. I traded my night shifts for lunch hours so I could spend my evenings with him.

Marshall had quit working construction and gotten a job as a car salesman. I bought a brand-new car from him with my tip money, a fast Trans Am with a big engine and four on the floor, loaded with every option in the brochure. Marshall drove the Corvette, and I drove what we joked was the family car since it had a trunk and a backseat.

One night, I was dreaming out loud of our future idyllic life together. I thought my options after Playboy were limited without a college degree or technical training, and I had no desire to go back for more education. Maybe I'd work as an Avon Lady or a Welcome Wagon representative while Marshall built his empire. "When we get married," I said, "do you think you want to stay right in town or live closer to your folks?"

His response was a dose of cold reality: "Well, you're still going to have to work, so we should probably live here, close to the highway."

What! Stay here? I looked around. Though I paid half of the rent, everything in the house was his. The heavy, manly leather furniture, the huge TV, the dark wood lamps, even the pictures on the wall. I was the renter, Marshall was the resident.

I tried even harder to be lovable. My plan was to be even more accommodating so that he could see how much he wanted me. Turns out, you can't build a relationship on sex. I gave in to his urging to introduce fantasy into our bedroom. He brought home explicit magazines and movies, and I participated in role-playing scenes for and with him. At first it was exciting—it heightened the experience. For a while. Soon, I felt like I was invisible. The very thing I was using to ingratiate myself to Marshall was actually objectifying me. I hated it.

"Why can't we just be us tonight?" I'd ask.

"It's not as good. Come on, you'll be okay once we get going, right? You always are."

Marshall's drinking increased. Eventually, the sooner he had a drink or two in him, the better the evening was. Sometimes he would drink so much he wasn't interested in having sex. I began to look forward to that.

Our conversations became compulsory.

"Will you be home for dinner?"

"Did you pay the water bill?"

"Is my coat at the dry cleaner's?"

"Your mother called. She wants to know if you'll look at her car."

I started picking up night shifts at the Club to avoid being at home. I worked doubles; I stayed in the dorm. "Hey, Marshall. I'm just about to start my second shift. I'm sure I'll be too tired to drive home tonight, and I have to be back for an early shift in the morning. Just letting you know I'm staying here."

"Sure, that's fine. I'm just going out for a few tonight anyway."

⚜

One evening at home, I held up a cigarette butt with lipstick on it. "Who's been here?" I demanded.

"That's yours."

"It's not my brand, and it isn't my lipstick."

"Oh. Well, Maura stopped over. Maybe it's hers."

"Did she use my towel too?"

"Yeah, I guess so. She needed to clean up before she left."

Angry, hurt, losing control, I shouted, "How could you do this? With a friend of mine? In our house?"

Nothing but silence. No eye contact.

I calmed myself. "What are we doing?" I asked quietly. "Do you even want to try anymore?"

His continued silence was my answer.

I was heartbroken. Not because Marshall had cheated on me, but because my dream for happily-ever-after had eluded me.

It was time to move out and move on.

Chapter 3

HOT & HUNKY

When Marshall and I imploded, I called my friend Jay Andraszczyk. He was there the next day with a moving van.

Jay and I met the fall of 1975, our freshman year of college, when he tromped into the dining hall with the rest of the varsity football team. He would tell you that he fell in love with me the first moment he saw me—that his knees went weak and his brain ceased to function at the sight of me. The place was all but deserted at that time of night, and the players pushed through the cafeteria lines, mounding piles of food on their serving trays, some of them not even bothering with plates, noisily recounting the highlights of their practice. Clean-cut, Jay looked like a lot of the other football players, at least those who hadn't yet broken their noses. He was hunky—broad through the shoulders with sturdy arms and legs, a round butt, and big hands. Instead of joining the other players, Jay casually slid his tray onto my table.

I thought, *Here it comes. I hope his line is imaginative.* I waited. He never even asked my name. In fact, instead of dazzling me with a clever pick-up line or even bragging about his accomplishments on the football field, the best he could summon was a quick smile and a mumbled, "Pass the salt, please."

While I waited for him to deliver the clever come-on that never arrived, I began to wonder if maybe he felt sorry for me, sitting alone in the dining hall, doing my best to look like I wanted to be there, which I didn't.

The only reason I was even at the university was that my mom, a *big* believer that education equaled opportunity, insisted on it. Mom wanted me to be degreed and credentialed so I could pursue any dream I wanted.

With my looks and body, combined with my fascination with men, she knew there was a risk that I'd end up in a job wearing skimpy clothes—or even no clothes. I spent many nights of my senior year of high school dancing in nightclubs and discotheques. I loved dancing—and I was a natural. I had great moves and beautiful lines. I could dance artistically or enticingly; it all depended on the partner.

Occasionally at those night spots I would be approached by a strip club owner or manager out on the town. They would ask me about dancing at their clubs, assuring me that I wouldn't have to dance (completely) nude and that I would make great money. Though flattered and curious, I always passed, but that didn't keep them from asking again and again. My mom intercepted one such telephone call asking me to take a shift at a well-known gentleman's club whose name she recognized immediately without ever having been inside. That was one message she didn't pass along. Stripping was a "Plan B" she didn't want explored.

I was lukewarm at best about going to college, but it was time for a fresh start. Earlier that year, Buzz, my first love and my first lover, had died when he smashed his car into a telephone pole at sixty miles an hour trying to go airborne over some railroad tracks. I sought solace with a charming alcoholic named Brandon who was manipulative and unpredictable. When he drank, his words were ugly and his actions were hurtful. Our breakup was messy. So, as you would redirect a toddler away from a hot oven door, my mom redirected me off to college and away from lousy boyfriends and neon signs advertising exotic dancers.

That's where Jay found me that night in the dining hall: hours away from home, miserable and lonely, eating my way out of sorrow.

Undaunted by his first failed attempt to dazzle me with his table manners, he came to the girls' dorm one night with a couple of his buddies, bouncing paddle balls, counting the sequential slaps—*and*, he pointed out, simultaneously chewing gum. "It's not as easy as I make it look," he said, laughing.

Jay was great—always fun, always polite. But I never thought of him as boyfriend material. If anything, he was more like the security-blanket friend snotty girls like me kept hanging around in case they need a favor.

Jay was a Christian, and while I didn't know any other Christians, from what I had heard in general and seen on *60 Minutes*, I was pretty sure they weren't allowed to have any fun. They couldn't go to movies or out dancing. The mental image I had of Christian women was that they had to wear dowdy clothes and ugly, thick-soled, flat shoes, maybe even a doily on their heads. They were forced to have huge families, and three or four generations lived together in communes—maybe even in the same house. None of this sounded the least bit interesting to me.

At first Jay's preposterously outdated standards seemed to confirm that mental image. He didn't drink or smoke or sleep around, although he didn't judge me for doing all those things. But as I got to know Jay, and as he talked openly about God and about his faith in Jesus Christ, he wasn't at all what I had expected Christians to be like—all pious and stodgy. He went to movies and came dancing with us; in fact, Jay and I won several local dance contests. He had an orange, souped-up Nova. As he spun the tires, doing doughnuts, I would scream, clinging to the passenger door. To show off, he would scoot to the center of the front seat and drive from there. He won money to pay for gas and parts by street racing.

He made friends with scholastic nerdy types, gym jockeys, and girls. And the girls loved him because he was so playfully flirtatious. He wasn't one of those creepy guys who hung all over you, invading your space.

Halfway through the second semester, a chance conversation with him revealed that he was, of all things, a virgin. My hot and hunky, witty, talented, intelligent friend had never had sex! And he didn't even have the good sense to be embarrassed about it! *Poor thing*, I thought. So out of charity and genuine appreciation for the many times he had come to my aid when I had been stranded at frat parties and needed a ride home, I offered to fill in the gaps of his missing experience.

He gently but firmly declined.

I couldn't understand it! This virtuous football player just wanted my company. I didn't know how to act. Off-balance and unwilling to take no for an answer, I orchestrated an elaborate scheme to seduce him and show him what he was missing.

A snowstorm provided the perfect opportunity. We were together in a dorm room. Alone. Stranded. For several nighttime hours. My legs were shaved and my undergarments were lovely. We talked for hours, avoiding the elephant in the room.

Finally, it was time to make my move. "I'm having such a good time," I said, "but I think it's time we went to bed."

Jay looked at his watch and nodded. "It's later than I thought. Yeah, I guess we should."

"So how do you want to do this?" I asked. What I meant was: Did he want the lights on so he could watch me undress? Was he so nervous he preferred total darkness?

"Oh," he said, pretending not to understand my meaning. "Where do you want to sleep—between the sheet and the sheet, or between the sheet and the blanket?"

I was crushed.

Rejected and embarrassed, I avoided Jay for a while, instead hanging out with like-minded girls who made me feel better about my own behavior with frat boys. But Jay was always there, never judging, rescuing me again and again from ugly situations I had misjudged. He would be the one to pick me up when my date passed out, leaving me stranded. He would be the one to take me to the ER when my date got too rough. He was only a call away—and knowing that he would always come for me gave me the courage to venture further and further away from my abysmal studies.

As my friend, Jay offered advice about the guys I dated. There was always something wrong with them in his view, and he had a point. I usually attracted cavemen or control freaks, both of whom show well at first and then deteriorate into danger. Jay wanted more for me than I wanted for myself.

We stayed in touch after I left Whitewater. He even visited me at the Playboy Club a couple of times. Jay had a pilot friend, Craig, who would fly him in for quick visits, using the airstrip on the Club property. I would set Craig up with one of my friends and we'd go out dancing or to a show.

It was still clear to both of us that he cared for me in a way I did not return. When I told him I was planning to move out of the Bunny Dorm to live with Marshall, his response was just what I'd expected: "That's about the *worst* thing you could do. Bad idea, Robyn. He's not good for you."

"I'm not a child, Jay," I said. "I know exactly what I'm doing."

Jay withdrew from me completely while Marshall and I lived together.

When I called to tell him he'd been right, that moving in with Marshall had been a big mistake and that I was moving into an apartment, he didn't say *I told you so*—he just came to get me. He moved me out of Marshall's house and into an attic apartment I'd found in Delavan, a small town closer to the Playboy Club.

The place was perfect. I could pay the rent with a couple night's tips. Every room in the little apartment had slanted ceilings. The ceilings in the kitchen were so sloped that I had to bow my head to wash dishes. The stove and refrigerator were just a smidge bigger than dollhouse replicas, but there was room for a small table and two chairs next to the window that looked out over the yard. The rear exit in the kitchen opened onto a small wooden deck from which a set of wooden stairs descended to the backyard and the one-stall garage, used for storage by the downstairs tenants. The cupboard doors were painted a cheerful canary yellow with shiny enamel and the frames were white like the appliances.

The living room was smaller than the kitchen, and I opted for two chairs instead of a couch, a deliberate reminder to myself that this new home was not for entertaining. I had a ten-inch portable black-and-white TV that sat on a little bookcase against the wall it shared with the bedroom. I bought a massive mahogany bedframe at an estate sale. It needed to be refinished, but I left it in its distressed condition, partly because I didn't have any experience refinishing furniture and partly because I felt as banged up as the headboard looked. When I put the box spring and mattress on the frame, the top of the mattress came to my waist. It felt royal. The bathroom had the same issue with the roofline; the ceiling wasn't high enough to stand in, so no shower, just a tub, but Jay hooked up a hose on a hook with a shower head so I could take kneeling showers.

I was like a big girl playing house. It was the first time I'd lived all on my own. I didn't have to accommodate anyone else's clothes or habits or style. My little apartment was just for me. I liked the quiet. I read a lot: historical fiction, autobiographies, and trashy entertainment magazines. The place was always clean.

My little house was in a nice working-class neighborhood. The couple downstairs were married, hardworking folks trying to have a baby. Pizza was delivered by a high schooler trying to make extra money for dates and gas. It was reminiscent of the little town of Lodi, where I'd spent my summers growing up. Main Street was lined with little shops and people waved at you, even if they didn't know you.

Jay and I dated a couple of times after the move—real dates, where he comes to the door, takes me out for dinner or a movie, then returns me home safe and sound. One night, long after he'd dropped me off, he called me.

"Hi," I said. "Didn't you just leave here an hour ago? Do you miss me already?"

"I do miss you. Why don't you quit Playboy, marry me, and let me take care of you?"

"Just like that? And give up all this?"

"You wouldn't have to work at that place anymore."

"Sounds heavenly—we could live on love," I said, laughing. "Ask me again when you get a real job." I was only partly teasing. He was working two part-time jobs while he finished up his degree at Whitewater.

"Okay, I will. But it's a standing offer, Robyn. I mean it."

"You made my night," I said. He was serious, but I pretended he was being playful. I knew he was testing my reaction, and I didn't want to give him false hope. I did so love to be with him, but that Christian thing was a deal breaker. He made me feel terrific and ashamed at the same time. I felt indebted to him for his chivalrous rescues and was willing to reward him in the best way I knew how, but he was looking for more than thank-you sex and knew that if he slept with me, I'd be gone. My obligation to him would have been fulfilled, and I'd be off.

Chapter 4

JUST SAY YES

"What the ... I asked for Friday night off!" Bunny Stella complained as she looked at the new schedule. "Now I have to find someone to take this shift!"

"Whatcha got?" I asked.

"Bunny Hutch."

Silence throughout the dressing room. The Bunny Hutch was the discotheque, and it wasn't considered a premier shift by anyone. I had been at Playboy about two years and was glad that I was all but done working that room. I didn't make eye contact with her.

"What do you have on Friday, Corey?" Stella asked my image in the bank of mirrors.

My reflection answered hers. "I'm working a lunch shift in the Playboy Club."

"Would you *pleeeeease* work my shift for me?"

"Ouch. No thanks—see if you can find someone else."

"Everyone is scheduled! I'll pay you to take it!"

"You must have something really special going on."

"Yeah, my sister's getting married in Chicago."

"Oh, that's too bad. But I really don't—"

"Please, Corey. I'll pay you fifty dollars."

"That hardly makes it worth it ... but okay, I'll work the stinkin' double."

"Great, thanks," she said as she peeled off a Ulysses S. Grant and handed it to me.

The Bunny Hutch disco was my least favorite room to work. It wasn't the atmosphere—it was that working the Bunny Hutch was sort of a low-girl-on-the-totem-pole assignment and I thought I was beyond it. I had reached the magic moment of seniority that mostly exempted me from the peon venues, including the Bunny Hutch. The hours there were long and the money could be mediocre. There was no food service— only dancing and cocktails. And lots of people got their own beverages from the bar. I loved the music and the dancing, but it was never a big money room for me. It was always noisy and overcrowded, so Bunnies usually had to cash out each order immediately instead of running up a tab that meant a good tip. I like collecting tips from an empty table after patrons left. I wasn't very good at lingering in anticipation of one. It felt like begging.

On the plus side, I spent nearly as much time dancing with patrons as I did hustling cocktails. I was still a fabulous dancer—that's how I got my first feature in the Best Bunnies layout of *Playboy* magazine. A Playboy photographer saw me dancing, submitted some shots to the magazine, and *voilà*, I enjoyed my first fifteen minutes of fame. Felons and derelicts from all over the country wrote to me asking for a personal performance. My mother was *so* proud.

Halfway through the shift that night, I recognized two men from the town of Lake Geneva. Bob was a bar owner and the ex-boyfriend of the Bunny of the Year, Bunny Jill, and she was still protective of that relationship. The other was Ron, an ex-con who occasionally worked for Bob. Ron was the on-again, off-again boyfriend of another of the senior Bunnies, Bunny Peggy. She had been there years longer than I had, with established friendships with the Bunny Mother and most of the room captains, all of whom could make life miserable for me. Other foolish Bunnies who had casually dated either Bob or Ron had been asked rather unpleasantly to stay away from him in the future. When they complained to me about it, I would say, "Good manners taught me not to make big stinky messes in my own backyard. You should do the same."

Ron hardly ever came to the Club, so I figured he was there to keep Bob from looking creepy as he scoped out the new girls. Neither of these men was strong on fidelity. Or for that matter, subtlety. I knew about their traditions of "checking out" and "breaking in" new Bunnies.

Since it was predominantly new bunnies who were scheduled in the Bunny Hutch, I assumed the two men were there to check out either the girl I was working with or the one I was substituting for. I figured I had been at Playboy too long to be of any interest to either of them. But I was wrong. Ron was there for me.

"What are you two up to tonight? Is it slow downtown?" I smiled my professional Bunny smile as I set down cocktail napkins.

"We're here to see you," said Bob.

"Really," I said sarcastically, still smiling with my mouth, but not my eyes. "That's hard to believe."

"No, we are. My friend Ron here has been wanting to meet you for a while."

I looked at Ron. He grinned at me, all the way up to the crinkles around his brown eyes. Bob kept talking, "Sure, he thought maybe you two could get a drink later."

Oh, no, no, no, I thought. *I know who your girlfriend is, and she is not to be trifled with.* But what I said was, "Sorry, I have a boyfriend."

Ron shook his head. "I don't think so. That guy screwed up and you moved out."

"Where did you hear that?" I asked.

"Oh, I know a lot about you," said Ron with another crinkly-eyed grin.

"Ron here has been interested in you for a long time," Bob said. "And now that you're not a couple anymore—well, the timing seems good for the two of you."

This is crazy, I thought. *They probably just wandered in here out of boredom or looking for Stella. Maybe Ron lost some kind of bet. Maybe I am the bet!*

I took their order. Ron ordered coffee. Interesting. "You don't drink?" I asked.

"Can't afford to dull my cat-like reflexes."

They hung around for another hour before they settled up to leave. "What about it—meet me downtown later?" Ron asked.

"Not tonight," I said, and then like an idiot I added, "I have to close tonight, so I can't make it." Sounding like I wanted to go but had a conflict with my schedule.

Then he asked, "How about tomorrow?"

"Let me think about it." *Aaaaggggghhhhh!* What was there to think about? Meet him and get the stink-eye or worse from Bunny Peggy? No, I didn't need to get into a pissing contest with her! And for what? A one-night stand? Unh-uh. Not worth it.

But I was intrigued.

Ron had quite a wild reputation.

He was an ex-con who had finagled residence in Lake Geneva as part of his parole after serving seven years in Joliet State Penitentiary for armed robbery. At least that's what they convicted him of; I'm sure there was much more that couldn't be proven. He had been in and out of trouble since middle school. He had ridden with the Chicago Outlaws Motorcycle Club for a while, surviving in a culture that created its own morality. He had convinced the parole board at Joliet that returning to his old haunts in Chicago would be dangerous for him and for society, and that the hamlet of Lake Geneva would be the best spot for a fresh start.

In Lake Geneva, Ron worked as a bartender and as a bouncer. He also worked on occasion for drug dealers as a guard or collecting debts. He handled drunks with street skill and discretion. If a man got drunk and out of line, Ron would escort him, forcibly if necessary, to the exit. If a woman got drunk or high, he would make sure she got to a place of safety—especially if she belonged to someone important.

Ron had dark eyes and an intimidating gaze that seemed to assess your strengths and weaknesses. He carried a blackjack in his boot, his fists were big, and his punch was powerful. In prison, he had spent considerable time in the weight room, bodybuilding. His body was bronzed and beastly powerful—but unlike the magazine bodybuilders, Ron was covered with scars and tattoos. He had a perfect smile, but not from orthodontia; he wore dentures up and a partial down. The missing teeth had been knocked out by a prison guard's stick at Joliet. He had dark brown hair that curled when it got longer than his collar, and he was always pushing it out of his eyes with both hands, especially when he came out of the water. He loved the water, and his scuba-diving equipment was among the few personal belongings he kept. Ron wanted to treasure hunt and dreamed of finding sunken ships full of treasure or of historical significance. He talked of going to Hawaii to dive in the turquoise ocean, but for the time being, he dove in the waters of Lake Geneva.

After that first visit to the Bunny Hutch, he turned up on many of my shifts and positioned himself in my station. Bunny Peggy had not been a friend of mine even before Ron started to pay attention to me, and it made for some awkward moments in the locker room. She still considered him her territory and wasn't interested in competition. Even though they weren't an official couple anymore—at least in his view—it was apparent that she didn't want to let go. I tried to keep the peace, mostly by keeping my distance, but she was hurt and that makes people say ugly things to you and about you.

None of that mattered after Ron presented me with a diamond solitaire engagement ring. The proposal came without much fanfare. Sitting on a dock, overlooking Lake Geneva, waiting for the sun to set, Ron held out a small white box. Wearing an expectant look, he opened the box to reveal the engagement ring. He proposed without saying a word. But I said, "Yes!" I was finally on my way to happily-ever-after.

I couldn't wait to show my mom. As we drove up to her house, she saw us and waved excitedly from the front window. She froze mid-wave when she saw the ring on my finger. Her face fell. That look said it all: How could I possibly want to marry Ron the Con?

I admit it—I knew from the beginning that we weren't a good match. There wasn't much common ground. But Ron was so compellingly dangerous that I felt safe and completely desirable. I wanted a man who was wholly devoted to me. Captivated, even. I was thrilled with the big diamond ring, and I liked that people were frightened of him. He wanted me, but just as much, he wanted the life I came from. He thought marrying me would usher him into my world—not Playboy, but my life outside of and before Playboy. I came from a long line of responsible and highly educated Midwesterners. You might have thought that, given his background, he would find "normal" kind of boring. But he wanted it. He liked that I was smart as much as he liked that I was pretty. He liked that I didn't drink to get drunk and that he had never had to pour me into someone else's car to be taken home. He liked that I only used drugs occasionally, to be social, like others have a glass of wine with dinner. Ron wanted to be respected and classy, as he perceived that I was, and thought if he married me it would come to him by association.

It was a pipe dream. Criminal record notwithstanding, he had no education beyond high school, and I don't think he'd even finished that. He had no occupational or vocational training aside from the streets and prison, making the kind of life I could step into on a moment's notice a long shot, at best, for him.

There is something recklessly confident about women like me who fall for the wrong men and think those men will change once they see how much we love them. We think these men will leave behind all the crazy and risky behavior that once attracted us to them and settle down to a life of civility and domestication. They will be genteel; they will become respected pillars of the community. But without divine intervention, the traditional life I came from and Ron aspired to was beyond our hope. Instead, there were guns and drugs and crazy people everywhere we lived.

What constitutes "normal" in life is relative, I suppose, contingent on the culture and the environment. And that's especially true when you don't know the absolute truth of God, and I surely did not. Still, I tried to believe that what I had was what I wanted, that it was a good thing to be married to an ex-con with specialized skills, to be a Bunny, to work till the wee hours of the morning, go out after, continue to dance and socialize while waiting for Ron to finish his shift as a bartender or peacekeeper, sleep late, and start all over again. There was routine but no stability, and our life together fast became what neither of us wanted.

After the wedding, which was held in the bar area of the Playboy Ski Chalet, with little pomp and less tradition, Ron moved into my couchless apartment sanctuary and promptly brought home a huge overstuffed sectional. He set up a weight room in the garage and started working out. He ate protein and drank raw eggs. He wanted to look different and to *be* different, to get healthy. His body morphed magnificently. The teen boys in the neighborhood would come over just to watch him lift. He quit the nighttime work and got a job as a foreman in a paint and body shop; I worked more day shifts at Playboy. He swore off cocaine; I cooked dinners.

It didn't take. It became intensely frustrating. Ron didn't know how to manage the people he supervised at work, and I didn't know how to encourage him to try something else. How do you ask a man who can barely read to go back to school so he can become someone he won't recognize and maybe won't even like?

The charm of the apartment stifled him. After a few months, he moved out. Apparently, forever is four months long.

But if nothing else, I am determined. And I'm a perfectionist. I didn't want DIVORCED as part of my biography, and I didn't want to hear "I told you so" from anyone. We went to marriage counselors—for months, with very little forward progress. Probably because I was so relentless, Ron finally agreed to try again. We rented a house in Lake Geneva and got a dog.

I may not have wanted to be divorced, but I was miserable being married, and so was he. I belittled him with sarcastic witticisms, lorded over him the vocabulary my mother had drilled into me, and attacked his lack of business acumen when he attempted to start up a salvage business on Lake Geneva. Often, boats swamped by storms would need to be retrieved or cars would careen into the lake and need to be hauled up. Sometimes a snowmobile would take a plunge through the ice and need to be hoisted to the surface. Ron, an accomplished diver, could do those things, but he had no skill at building relationships with owners of lakeshore houses, or with the Coast Guard, and had at best a wary truce with the police department. Consequently, he was rarely called.

Arguing about money got heated. I didn't want to be our sole support, and he really didn't want to work nights again. Our arguing escalated until one night his contempt grew beyond his ability to verbalize. I could see it in his posture and his eyes. I was so scared, but I was too stubborn or too proud to back down. I stood firm, and he came closer. I could see in his eyes that he was going to hit me, and I fainted dead away.

I woke up on the kitchen floor, right where I had been standing. Ron was gone, but he soon returned, and we both pretended the thing that had almost happened, hadn't happened.

I had been at Playboy nearly four years when Ron announced that he was considering offering his services to the FBI to crack down on drug traffic. We argued. I didn't believe it was a matter of conscience or repentance. I thought it was his newest plan to gain entrance to a professional world outside his educational and experiential reach. I mocked his idea in the most confrontational and unflattering ways.

He lost his temper and hit me. The force sent me tumbling over the coffee table, glasses flipped and splashed on the carpet, ashtrays dumped. I thudded against the opposite wall.

Did he hit me out of frustration with me, with our situation, with his feeling of being trapped? I don't know, but I do know that even in his anger, he exercised self-control. I know that because, despite his incredible strength and skill with his fists, I lived. And because he only hit me once. It sent me reeling, but left me relatively undamaged.

He stood frozen as I got up. It was done. That was the deal breaker and we both knew it. If I stayed, it would only get worse. If I stayed, I was going to die.

Again, we pretended that everything went back to normal for us, even as I plotted my escape. I told him I needed to go home for an extended visit. I gave my notice at Playboy, but asked the Bunny Mother to keep my resignation a secret. I was scared.

I knew being a Bunny is not a career; it's a job. No one retires from being a Bunny. You either quit or get fired for losing your Bunny Image, and while I wasn't in any immediate danger of losing my image, I was tired of changing my clothes. Get up, get dressed, go to work, get undressed, get into uniform, work your smiling shift, get out of uniform, get dressed, go home, get undressed, get dressed in clubbing clothes, go out, go home, get undressed, go to bed, sleep, and start all over.

I packed my clothes, sneaked my grandmother's dishes into the trunk of my car, and ran away.

In the safety of my mother's home, surrounded by educators and professionals, my head cleared. I was normal again. I read the newspaper and wore the same outfit all day.

I decided to go back to school to become a teacher. But I was married to a man who couldn't make that journey with me. I didn't know what to do about that. I was terribly conflicted. Should I try once more?

Seeing my struggle, my mother said, "Robyn, I think you have tried everything you can. You've suffered enough. Let him go."

That settled it for me. I would shed my marriage, my husband, my connections to the past, and start over.

If only it were so easy.

When it became obvious to Ron that I wasn't coming back to Lake Geneva and that I wasn't inviting him to join me in Madison, we met a couple of times to talk it over. When I was with him, I just wanted to try again, to forget about the divorce. Then I would walk back into my mother's house and my resolve would harden. Ron wasn't going to morph into someone he wasn't, and I couldn't fix all that was wrong with us. I had lost respect for him, leaving me with only feelings of compassion and pity. I was miserable and he was angry. Our marriage was fatally wounded, so we let it agonizingly bleed out.

I filed for divorce and cried. I enrolled in college at Madison and cried. I went out with girlfriends and I cried. I cried because I was still married and wanted my freedom, and I cried because I thought I should never have married Ron in the first place and hated being so mean to him. Some days I cried because my marriage had failed and I still wanted to be with him.

Insanity is doing the same thing again and again, expecting different results. My insanity was dating during the process of divorce to medicate the pain of loss and loneliness. The attention of lots of men supplied a "fix" that made me feel wonderful. I wasn't very good at being married, but I was a pro at dating. I turned it into a dangerous game: How many men could I juggle at the same time? I catalogued what I wore with whom on what type of date, along with the gist of the conversation, so that I wouldn't duplicate outfits or anecdotes. I documented any romantic or sexual activity and scored the creativity and competency of the partner. I was desperate for the grand prizes of acceptance and fulfillment, and I thought perhaps they were waiting in the arms of another man.

At night, on the town, I felt no pain. In the morning, I was swallowed up by guilt and discouragement. I didn't know how I was going to break the cycle. Maybe I needed different contestants for my game.

I remembered how special Jay, that Hot and Hunky football player from college, had always made me feel. I decided to give him a call.

He was surprisingly glad to hear from me.

His mother was *not*!

Chapter 5

SECOND TIME'S A CHARM

Jay and his dad, Andy, sat watching television after dinner. The local newscast ended and the music cued for *PM Magazine*, a thirty-minute entertainment program that featured juicy items of local interest. My smiling face flashed across the screen as the announcer urged viewers to stay tuned for a look at the new Playboy Bunny costume being premiered at Lake Geneva's Cabaret Show Lounge. Jay lurched upright for a better look. Sure enough, as promised, there was a twelve-minute feature about the Playboy Bunnies of Lake Geneva. As a Training Bunny, I was part of the feature. Jay looked at his dad and said, "If I ever get another chance with her, I'm going to marry that girl!" His dad chuckled.

Two weeks later, I called the only number I still had for Jay, at his parents' home. Andy answered gruffly. He was evasive and terse when I asked how I might get in touch with Jay—until I told him who I was, and suddenly Andy became downright jovial. He told me he would be seeing Jay soon and would be sure to tell him I had called. He was still chuckling as he hung up the phone. I thought the whole conversation had been odd.

Later that night, the phone rang. "Hi, Robyn, it's Jay Andraszczsyk. My dad said you'd called. Are you visiting your mom?"

"Living with her, actually. I'm getting a divorce and hiding out at my mom's. Back in school. My mother's so relieved, even if I'm only taking gen. ed. classes toward a yet-to-be-determined degree. I bartend nights at a supper club in Middleton. They love having an ex-Bunny on the payroll. How are you?"

"Great. I'm living with my folks right now too. I help my mom out with her business and drive a school bus."

"Making the most of your college education, I see?"

"Yeah, I took a little detour and had to move back home to regroup. Plus, my mom really needed the help."

"Gotta like a guy who takes care of his mother. Hey, if you're ever in Madison, look me up."

"My schedule is pretty tight, but I'll call you soon."

He called two hours later and said he had cleared some time and would like to take me out for dinner and to catch up. He showed up the next night in a three-piece suit with candy for me and flowers for my mom. He chatted casually with her about current events, disagreeing pleasantly about political candidates, and quoted some obscure litera-ture, totally impressing both my mom and me. Throughout the evening, he held every door and chair for me, stood up when I went to the ladies' room and again when I returned.

I prattled on and on about how challenging it was—or rather, had been—to be married, and how depressing it was to be getting divorced. "I'm probably doomed," I said, "to spend my life either alone or bouncing from one man's arm and bed to another, because I'm so bad at choosing men for anything more than accessorizing an event."

"That's nonsense," he said. "God loves you, Robyn. He wants more for you than that. *I* want more for you than that!"

"I don't know, Jay. My track record stinks."

"That's because you don't choose well. It would be a shame for you to settle for less than a man who would die for you." He spoke with author-ity and conviction. I wanted to believe him.

The conversation moved on. "Doing any dancing now that you're back home?" he asked.

"Some, but I can't find a decent partner," I teased.

"I can fix that."

SECOND TIME'S A CHARM

"I'd like that."

We talked about college days, frat parties, and bad dates. About the dance contests we had won and the times we'd skipped class to go for joyrides and how many times we had not gotten nearly enough sleep or enough studying done for class.

"So what are you doing now?" I asked. "I haven't heard anything about you for years."

"I don't keep in touch with married women I'm in love with."

"Right."

He paused, then continued. "I blew my knee out my junior year. I had surgery, but it ended my football career."

I knew Jay well enough to know what a blow that must have been. He had spent zillions of hours on practice fields, in training camps, and running the country roads around his house—all working toward his dream of playing pro football, preferably for the Green Bay Packers. He'd suited up as a little tike and had trained relentlessly ever since. After his record-setting career in high school, college recruiters had shown up offering scholarships to universities and colleges. He'd started every game as a freshman at U.W. Whitewater, making big plays that kept him in the lineup. Jay played center; he was as quick and agile as he was strong and disciplined—due in large part to the superior gene pool he'd inherited from his undefeated boxing champion father and from his own tenacious training regime. Upside down and backward, he could thread a football through the center of a hanging tire from ten yards. He would entertain crowds and frustrate vendors at fairs and carnivals by snapping a football through his legs, sending it sailing through a tire at a midway game, winning huge stuffed animals.

"When I couldn't play anymore, I sort of lost my way. At first I was angry. I've always done what was expected of me. I never gave my parents any trouble, I followed the rules. I worked hard on and off the field. I thought I *deserved* to play pro ball. When I got hurt, I thought God had let me down."

"That must have been awful. Is that when you moved back home?"

"Nope, I finished school, but I decided I didn't care about pleasing a God who would let my dreams shatter." He kept his attention on his plate. "I thought I didn't have any future, so there was no longer anything to save myself for. Alcohol took the edge off, and then …" He lit a cigarette and then continued. "I moved to Chicago and worked for a family there, doing things."

"What things?"

"I'd rather not say. Let's just say I'm not very proud of what I did there." Silence lingered. He took another drag on his cigarette.

"There was a woman too. She was married."

"Oh Jay." I couldn't imagine how my straightlaced Christian friend had ended up in Chicago doing who knows what—or that he had gotten involved with a married woman, no less. It made me sad for him—and yet I also felt relieved that the two of us were on more even moral ground.

"Yeah. I realized what a mess I had made, but I didn't know what to do. That's when I went home. My mom needed some help, so I moved back in with them. My folks have no idea about Chicago."

Back home in Hartland, Wisconsin, in the safety of his mom's love and her unwavering faith, Jay started over. He started back to church and found a forgiving Jesus. He was working on forgiving himself. He set aside the women and the drugs but couldn't quite shake the cigarettes. He still enjoyed the taste and effect of gin but indulged infrequently. His mom had an upholstery business in the big old barn behind the house, so she hired him to haul around heavy furniture, tear apart cushions, rip off old fabric, and repair the wooden frames of couches and chairs. Mindless work to keep his hands busy while he considered his options.

Aside from our true confessions and 20/20 hindsight, the evening was spent laughing and reminiscing. I was so comfortable with him; he had always made me feel like I was at home, like I could be myself. We laughed until my cheeks hurt. Before dessert was cleared, he got down on one knee in the restaurant and proposed, just like he had done two other times in the past.

"Sure," I said playfully. "Just as soon as I'm divorced."

When he took me home, he gave me a big hug and a little kiss on the cheek and left.

The next morning I canceled all the upcoming dates I had and tore up their scorecards.

⚜

After that, Jay and I saw each other frequently even though we lived sixty miles apart. Three weeks after our first date, he came to the house looking serious and determined. "We have to talk." *What now?* I thought. *He's come to tell me he's joined the Foreign Legion and is leaving next week? He's come to his senses and he's breaking up with me?*

In the little-girl bedroom my mom had created for me, he moved the Raggedy Ann doll out of the white rocking chair and put me in it, then he sat opposite me on the yellow-and-white-striped bedspread. He folded his hands tightly and looked at the floor for a long time. When he looked up, he said, "Robyn, I love you. My dance card is full, and your name is on every line. I'm asking you again to marry me. But if you say no this time, I'm walking out of your life forever and I won't be back."

I felt as if all the air in the room froze and everything in it was suspended in anticipation of my answer. I wasn't yet divorced from Ron. I wasn't finished with school. Jay didn't have a real job. Neither of us had any money set aside. My mother would *kill* me if I said yes.

And yet … there really wasn't anything to contemplate.

I said, "Yes."

I had filed for divorce, but the hearing was months away. Ron and I were still legally married, and I was terrified of him. I dreaded what he would do when he found out I was now engaged to someone else. Would he decide that if he couldn't be with me, no one else would either?

Jay wasn't the slightest bit concerned. He wasn't intimidated by Ron or his reputation. Fearless by nature and convinced that his experiences on and off the football field had made him Ron's equal in ferocity and fighting skill, he responded to my fears with a look that indicated he'd seen it all before and wasn't the least bit worried. I thought we'd both die, but I decided to trust Jay.

I announced to the other formidable force in my life, my mother, that we were engaged. As I expected, she was seething mad. In the short time she had spent with Jay, she'd decided that she liked him—but all this Christian stuff might as well have been voodoo to her. "It's too soon," she said. "It's too fast," she said. "What do you know about him, his family, his religion?" she said. "I don't want you joining a cult!"

When reasoning didn't work, she told me if I married Jay she would cut me off. I would be out of the will and off her Christmas list. This was new territory—I had never heard her threaten me before. But I had seen her take strong positions with her staff, with my teachers, and with her boyfriends. My mom wasn't afraid of engaging in battle to get to a better solution, and she didn't often lose.

And she was rarely wrong.

So I backpedaled with Jay, telling him that my mommy thought we should slow down or else. "She isn't trying to punish me—she's just trying to protect us from making a mistake, to give us time to make sure," I explained.

"I *am* sure. Absolutely sure," he said. "I have loved you completely for six years. We don't need her money, and while I would appreciate her approval, I can live without it. Besides, I think she'll back off her threats if you stand firm."

As horrible as it felt, I told Mama I was as sure of my decision as I had ever been of anything (which wasn't saying much). I told her I didn't want her money but I needed her blessing. She must have concluded that she couldn't fix what I didn't think was broken—or maybe she had finally decided that Jay and I might actually make it. Most likely, she had decided to look for alternative ways to sabotage my choice later. For whatever reason, she softened.

Jay and I continued to see each other and talk on the phone. Our phone bills were outrageous. He paid for all of them. He paid for my car insurance, all our dates, most of my gasoline, and all of his. What he couldn't cover with the paychecks from the new job he'd taken at McGraw-Hill as a sales rep, he made up for by pawning jewelry, musical instruments, and sports equipment.

Heroic men in love do crazy things. A snowstorm blew through

Madison one wintry night and dumped a foot of snow while I was at my bartending job. Jay drove sixty miles through the storm to drive me the four miles home, then slept on Mom's couch till 4:00 a.m. and drove back home through the dark, snow-drifted highway roads to work the next day. That kind of chivalry—foolish as it was—was not lost on my mom.

It was time for me to meet his parents. They lived out in the country, near Milwaukee. I pulled into their driveway, parked my car, looked in the mirror to check my lipstick—and just as I turned to open the door, two huge Doberman pinschers bounded up to the car, barking as if I were a treed animal. Ziggy was Jay's dog, and Oscar was his parents'. They jumped up and put both front paws on the car door, their big black barking heads face-to-face with mine through the glass. I wanted to start the car and burn rubber out of there, but Jay came calmly out of the house and commanded them into submission. I still wasn't eager to leave the safety of the car, but he opened the door and extended his hand.

His parents were hospitable, but so different from my family. They shouted to each other from room to room, the table talk was boisterous and rough (but not coarse), and they *lived* in their house. I mean they used their home as if it were actually a place to enjoy and relax—not pristine and sterile like my mom's home. There were water spots and soap splatters around the sinks and the pillows on the couch were randomly tossed about. There was a thin layer of dust on each of the ten thousand figurines, delicate teacups and saucers, and other knickknacks that seemed to cover every surface that wasn't already occupied by a Bible or religious book. The busy wallpaper in the dining room was hidden behind a collage of framed faces bearing the same genetic coding. It was comfortable.

After supper, Jay sat at the counter in the kitchen and I rocked in a chair too short for my long legs. Jay's mom, Helen, stood by the kitchen sink in her country kitchen. "You mean you never once been to church?" she asked in her distinctive Louisiana drawl.

"Well, sure, I've been to church—you know, Christmas Eve and funerals and stuff."

"Mom is at church every time the doors are open," Jay said. "Reads the Bible every day." I thought I detected a hint of pride in his voice.

"I don't know much about the Bible," I said. "I suppose there is a Superior Being somewhere, but I just don't think about it much."

"Well, I've been prayin' for you since my boy told me 'bout you!" she said, almost under her breath.

I thought, sincerely, *Isn't that nice of her!* I hadn't yet grasped that her fears concerning our marriage matched the level of foreboding my mom had, but for different reasons. My mom didn't want me marrying a religious fanatic who would brainwash me. Helen didn't want her son to marry a Jezebel, a heathen girl who had no idea how to love him like he deserved. She kept her opinions to herself, conveying little about her misgivings, knowing how stubborn and determined Jay was. She knew that I had been an unattainable desire of his for years, and that he would not be deterred.

Never a fan of big weddings, especially big church weddings, my mom announced (in what I suspect was another attempt to discourage us) that she would pay us to elope. Jay's mom and dad were committed to a church wedding. After all, they were Jesus people and it was Jay's first wedding. I was on board with the traditional church wedding idea. I pictured me in an almost-white dress and Jay in a black tux. I wanted big stained-glass windows, an aisle of flower petals, and lots of candles. I tried to enthuse Mom about that plan, but she said the only decision she would be making about the "ordeal" was what dress she personally would be wearing and not to count on her for anything beyond that. To help finance our reception, she gave us the one thousand dollars she would have shelled out for the elopement bribe.

Jay's family was all about the frou-frou, and they had connections for flowers and cakes and decorations. We found a church that looked storybook near his folks' home. The grounds were beautiful, and the small building was lousy with stained glass. After spending eighteen minutes with Jay and me to discuss the use of his church for our ceremony, the minister wouldn't marry us until we'd gone through premarital counseling with him. During the compulsory sessions, he forced us to talk about things that were uncomfortable to talk about: money, holiday traditions, God ... children.

It was awkward for me. Mostly, I wanted to control all the things I had always controlled but give the illusion of letting Jay have a say about them. One thing I did know, most emphatically, from the start: I did not want children. I agreed to marry Jay only on the condition that I *never* had to reproduce.

I had considered having a baby when I was married to Ron. I'd thought it was a good time for it, physiologically speaking—I was in my early twenties and healthy. Ron was thirteen years older than me, and if we waited too long, he'd be mistaken for grandpa at the kids' soccer games. Playboy offered outstanding medical insurance, and I was already used to being up all night. It was all very logical.

After the disintegration of that marriage and another bad ending to the dream of happily-ever-after, I viewed children as baggage that tied you to people you wanted nothing further to do with. Even though I had every intention that this marriage to Jay should go the distance, I still wanted to protect my escape route, and that meant no children. Moreover, I wanted Jay's undivided attention for myself, and babies are spotlight stealers. I thought if I remained Bunny beautiful, and didn't give up my hourglass figure and my four-inch heels due to some pregnancy, I could keep Jay focused on me. I told the minister and Jay that I wouldn't be upstaged by a baby. "He's not coming home and kissing some kid before he kisses me!"

Jay wanted children, but he wanted me more. He agreed to forgo a family in order to have me as his bride.

We got married the first weekend after my divorce was final. Both anxious mothers put on their game faces for the wedding. Helen smiled and cried and prayed. When I promised to love, honor, and *obey* Jay, I thought my mother's head would split wide open. She wore a fixed smile, a beige dress, and a paper badge that said MOTHER OF THE BRIDE.

My dad and Sandra (wife number three) drove in on their Gold Wing motorcycle. My dad was a working stiff. He painted houses and hung drywall for a living. He set his own hours so it wouldn't interfere with trout season or the opening day of deer hunting. He drove a fancy pickup truck with his name pinstriped in an elegant font on the door. It didn't advertise his business; it boasted ownership. He wore a green leisure suit, but at least he didn't wear the hideous cow-shaped, turquoise-and-mother-of-pearl-inlaid belt buckle he had been wearing when I'd told him about the wedding. I was relieved that he came at all.

There had been a heated discussion about how I would get down the aisle. When it was proposed that I be escorted by my father, my mom said if I couldn't make it down the aisle on my own then I shouldn't even be getting married, and that if anyone needed to "give me away," it was going to be her since she had been the one to raise me, sacrifice for me, provide for me, and protect me since their divorce when I was three years old. She wasn't about to let my dad swoop in and pretend he had done anything to prepare me for my wedding day or act like he'd paid for the wedding. The idea of having my mother walk me down the aisle was too weird even for me, so I walked the aisle alone. She was right; I didn't need help to get from one end of the church to the other.

The wedding pictures reflect a romantic affair. Everyone was smiling—except the minister, who wore a grimace much like one wears when you have acted against your better judgment but hope against all odds that the situation will turn out well anyway.

For the reception, we rented a quaint restaurant near the church. I chose it for the soft pink décor and a deck that wrapped around the side and rear of the building. The food was exceptional, and we ate and drank and smoked all afternoon. The weather cooperated, at least to the extent that it didn't rain, but it was hot and humid and wilted everyone's big, poufy hair.

There was no money for a honeymoon. We spent our first night together in the one-bedroom apartment Jay had rented for us in Waukesha, Wisconsin, close to his office. We were alone and married, and he'd turned up the heat in the waterbed for me to make sure conditions were ideal for the consummation of our marriage. The bed's heat worked well for the first hours of the evening's activities, but afterward, while I slept contentedly, Jay tossed and turned, finally waking up in a puddle of sweat long before dawn. He promptly dialed the bed's heat back to low.

The next night I woke up shivering. And so our married life began.

Chapter 6

MOVES AND SURPRISES

Six weeks after our wedding, McGraw-Hill transferred Jay to a territory in West Michigan. Frankly, I was delighted to be moving 350 miles away from well-intentioned but intrusive in-laws on both sides. Jay moved alone to Grand Rapids for five weeks of orientation while I wrapped up the secretarial job I had begged to be hired for two months earlier. He commuted five hours each way to be home with me every weekend, telling me about the city of Grand Rapids, the office where he worked, and the misery of living alone in a swanky hotel. I told him it wasn't much better where I was, thank you very much, living in an apartment close to no one I knew except his family, who felt free to drop in on me day or night just to say hello. I had no friends and got lost all the time. I could barely navigate to work and the grocery store—and heaven forbid that I hit a detour. I'd probably end up in Nebraska. Besides that, my boss was quite perturbed at my leaving so soon and made sure to tell me so every day. But Jay was too excited about his new adventure to pay much attention to my whining.

Then came the day the big green-and-yellow moving van swallowed up our furnishings, and we left Wisconsin for good. It took ten more days of easy living at the Harley Hotel before the van deposited our belongings into the sweet two-bedroom townhouse Jay had chosen for us in a huge low-income housing complex because it was clean and quiet. He must have looked at it during nap time, because we soon discovered we were flanked and outnumbered by families with children. Barbie Big Wheels and Tonka trucks clicked up and down the sidewalk in front of the place. Wee bikes with training wheels littered the postage-stamp-size patch of grass in front of each unit, and on weekends the munchkins were outside practically at dawn making too much racket to sleep through.

Being annoyed over the kids' noise was one of the few things we seemed to agree on. I liked to read; Jay liked to watch TV. I listened to country music; Jay was a classic rock enthusiast. I ate like a bird, and he ate like a Viking. I was neat and tidy, whisking away dirty dishes practically before Jay had a chance to take his last bite. He liked to linger over the plate and the newspaper, dressed down in yesterday's comfortable flannel shirt and sweatpants. Toilet seats and toothpaste caps, music preferences and waterbed temperatures were just the smoke of a smoldering blaze that would be the real test of our commitment to stay together. The hot zone of the fire was that he loved me more than I loved him, and we both knew it.

Jay was waiting for me to learn to love him without reservation. Unfortunately for Jay, I didn't know how to love him any differently. I had never been able to sustain a relationship, and I kept hearing the recording in my head that this thing I had with Jay was too good to be true. Sometimes I wanted to be cherished, protected, and taken care of. At other times I rebelled against being "kept."

I poured myself into finding a job. To justify having a say about house operations and finances, I thought I needed to contribute. And I wanted a safety net in case I needed it. I was afraid of losing my independence, and I was afraid of losing him. Jay didn't mind if I worked outside the house, although he would have been just as happy to have a stay-at-home wife.

I got a job managing a ladies' fitness salon where middle-aged women stood on belted machines that jiggled them while they chatted away to the woman on the next machine. Jay was performing well at McGraw-Hill, so we moved out of the townhouse, away from the noisy neighbor kids, and into a starter house: a two-story, two-bedroom, one-bathroom home on a corner lot.

It was the view from the front porch that sold us. The place across the street was an anomaly in the neighborhood. It was an estate, obviously built before the city of Grand Rapids burgeoned out to the domain of genteel country estates. It had been built by old money and its lot consumed the entire block. A gardener was employed to manage the lawn (which never sprouted so much as a single dandelion), the cherry trees (which bloomed so spectacularly they drew both amateur and professional photographers), and the flower beds, which were elegantly uniform. Underground sprinklers, a novelty in that neighborhood, sprayed glistening water in the late-afternoon sun. The imposing fence marking the estate's border was made up of monogrammed brick pillars every fifteen paces like sentries, strung together by two heavy black chains, adorned midway between the pillars by a bronze lion's head.

Neighborhood rumor had it that the mansion was occupied by one old lady, assisted by a rotating nursing staff. There were murmurs about a stipulation in the old man's will that required the widow to remain in the home or lose it, but it looked to me like no sacrifice to stay put. I loved that house, and I loved that I lived in its neighborhood. It was the marker by which directions to my place were given. I sat on the front porch of my little house, smoking cigarettes, staring at the manicured estate, trying to figure out a way to get a peek inside.

Our house, on the other hand, was a work in constant progress. Jay was a visionary. He saw tremendous possibilities in our house. Problem was, by the time he was 80 percent finished with one project, he would get bored and start a new one. We stripped woodwork, fixed windows, ripped up carpet, tore down walls, drywalled, painted, carpeted. It never ended. We started to lose our sense of humor.

Being surrounded by projects still 20 percent incomplete bothered me, but not as much as our first permanent houseguest: Ziggy. Jay had gotten the Doberman as a pup before we married and had taken the dog everywhere with him. The no-pet rule at the townhouse had given me a yearlong reprieve which I had taken for granted. When we moved into our own house, Jay wanted his dog back. I wanted to run his dog over with my car.

Ziggy contended for Jay's attention. He was expensive to maintain: food, shots, groomer, veterinarian—not to mention cleaning bills and repairs. He chewed clothing and furniture. He marked his territory. He barked and nipped at everyone—including me. His short hairs poked out of every fabric—clothing or furniture.

I hated that dog.

Every Christmas, we dutifully made the long trek back to Wisconsin to spend the holiday with family—and the best part about those visits was that the dreadful beast stayed with Jay's parents. Most years the weather was horrible, and the new energy-saving 55-mph speed limits really agitated Jay, who liked to drive like he was training for the Indy 500. I tried repeatedly sighing heavily to indicate my displeasure about his driving. I dramatically tightened my seat belt. He kept weaving in and out of traffic, jockeying for position that would get us to my mother's house fourteen seconds sooner. I decided to try a different approach: distract him with conversation.

"Do you think your folks will like the towels we got them?"

"*We* didn't get them towels. You did. There is nothing wrong with the towels they have. We spent way too much on gifts this year."

"Your mother loves our big fluffy towels. I was just trying to do something nice for her."

"No, you were trying to even the score because you bought your dad that expensive shirt and your mother that necklace. My folks don't care if we get them anything. They just want some time with us. You'd rather buy them a present they don't need than spend time with them."

The weaving in traffic continued. He missed the bumper of another car by an eyelash. I gasped loudly.

"Good God, Jay, you're going to kill us!"

"You're the one who has to visit your mother, so I'm taking you back. You should be happy."

I pouted for a while, then said, "While we're on the subject—you only give me a couple of days to see everyone. We don't go back to Wisconsin very often, and if I spend much time with your family, that doesn't leave enough time for me to see all *my* relatives."

I didn't want to come right out and say I didn't *like* being at his parents' house, with the big dogs and noisy people and surrounded by a chaos of knickknacks. Besides, it was easier for Jay. His family had formed a compound of sorts: His sister and her family lived next door to the parental unit, and his brother lived in a suite in the upstairs of his parents' home. For me to spend any time with my mom, brother, grandparents, aunts, uncles, and cousins, not to mention my dad, his mom, and my half-sister and their families, meant visiting multiple homes in half as many cities. I figured that, since I had so many stops to make, my family's share of the time should be double Jay's. He didn't agree. His solution was to drop me off at my mom's, spend an hour with her, then go to his folks' house until it was time to pick me up to return to Michigan.

He expected me to see the folly of being married but taking separate vacations, and then capitulate. Just like I expected him to.

"Robyn, I don't know why you insist on chasing your dad. If he really wanted to see you, he'd call *you*, or at least come and see you. He doesn't. If you haven't captured his heart by now, you're not going to do it with a shirt. He probably already has a dozen just like it. And as for the rest of your family, don't you think they'd understand if we divided the time we have between our families so we could stay together?"

He was right about my dad, of course. But I wanted to see my mama, even if I had to sacrifice our marital harmony to do it.

On one of those *married-but-visiting-separately* trips, the phone rang on Christmas Eve at my Grandma Clark's, where I was staying. It was Helen, Jay's mom. "Robyn," she drawled. Her voice sounded tired. "Jay didn't want me to call you, but he's been awful sick for days. I finally told him, 'You gotta go to the hospital, son!' Well, he didn't want to go, but he was in too much pain to argue, so Andy and I took him to the ER."

My husband's been sick for days and didn't bother to call me? This had better not be a ploy to wreck my family time or punish me for not spending the time at his mom's! It didn't occur to me that, just maybe, my behavior had been so selfish that he didn't think I'd care if he was in the hospital as long as I got my family holiday.

"The doctors think his appendix has burst and they gotta operate right away tonight. They don't know how much damage there is till they open him up. I thought you should know. You're his wife."

I was stunned. "What hospital is he in?"

Mom and I left immediately in her car to make the ninety-mile drive to the hospital. When we got there, Jay was still in the operating room.

Hours went by with no word. Andy and Helen waited in a different area from Mom and me. Praying, I suppose. I did some of that too.

Finally, the surgeon found me in the waiting room. "Jay is in recovery," he said. "He's lucky to be alive. His appendix had ruptured, and his belly was full of gangrenous infection. When blood can't travel freely throughout the body, infection develops, and tissue dies. That makes his condition extremely serious. Potentially life-threatening, in fact, since he wasn't treated quickly. We'll keep an eye on him and let you know when you can see him."

I wept. Why had Jay waited almost three days to go in? Why hadn't I been there? Would he live? Would he recover? Would he be the same?

When I was allowed to see Jay, I hardly recognized him. His skin was pasty and sallow, there were dark circles under his eyes—in fact, his facial skin looked like a corpse's. Tubes ran from bags on poles into his arms and under the covers. He opened his eyes, but there was no spark. He tried to reach his hand for me, but he didn't have the strength. There was only the tiniest curve at the side of his mouth, trying to let me know he was in there somewhere, fighting his way out of the infection that was trying to kill him.

I sat at Jay's bedside for days, leaving only when someone else spelled me.

Gradually, his color came back, and a little strength. He found his voice. "I want to go home," he whispered hoarsely.

He was on the mend.

I drove him back home to Grand Rapids in our car, but he really should have been transported in an ambulance. He took double doses of painkillers and reclined as much as the car seat would allow. I had never driven in Chicago traffic. No map, no GPS, no experience. Jay navigated me through the tollways and around the big lake. I was a nervous chauffeur, but we made it.

For months after the surgery, Jay had to keep the wound packed and open to allow healing from the deepest part of the incision up to the skin. His stubborn resistance to going to the hospital had left him scarred, nerve-damaged, temporarily disabled, and addicted to prescription painkillers. He was on leave from work, but I wasn't—nor did it occur to me to take time off to be with him. I also didn't see any problem with calling my mother to complain how hard my life was, having to take care of Jay—and to tell her about all of that horrible dog's naughty antics. I was completely unaware how unimportant that made Jay feel.

He was alone and in constant pain, despite three additional surgeries to correct the damage. At first he pounded narcotics, then finally weaned himself off them. Breaking free of that addiction left space for new ones. When he was finally able to return to work, he drank to celebrate big sales and he drank to commiserate lost ones. He smoked pot to relax and randomly looked at porn to escape. I cried and cajoled and whined. I posted "appropriate" Bible verses where he would see them; he tore them up.

It took a ticket for DWI to sober him up. He didn't go to jail or lose his job, but he had to pay a huge fine, hire an attorney, confess to his boss, and have a gizmo installed in his car that prevented ignition if he failed to accurately enter the start code before turning the key. He had a restricted license that allowed him to drive only for work-related reasons. It was humbling and infuriating for both of us. I had to drive us everywhere—and according to him, my driving was so bad it nearly drove him to start drinking again.

Things didn't improve much once he regained his driving privileges. During one heated argument, he yanked my wedding ring off my finger and told me he was sorry he'd ever given me his name. Another time he took my car keys and told me he was done taking care of me if I couldn't or wouldn't reciprocate with kindness and gratefulness. After each of those incidents, I would call my mother. And she would send me money for an attorney and a plane ticket back to Madison. I didn't contact a lawyer, but thinking it would be an incentive for Jay to be nicer or more patient, I *did* tell him my mom thought I should. Not a good idea. It made him so mad he left me on the side of the highway and told me to call *her* to pick me up.

I sat on the side of the road howling until he came back to get me. Which he did.

For my part, I played the victim, the martyr. I elicited sympathy and even praise for putting up with him.

I'm sure Jay questioned his sanity for marrying me, but he also held on to a vapor of hope that I might someday become the woman he saw the potential in me to be. I whimpered and wished the sweet man who had swept me off my feet would show up again in my husband.

It was dreadful. But we were stuck. Where was the loophole that would allow us to escape? I refused to have another divorce on my record. Jay *never* said the word *divorce* out loud, never threatened me with it. He had his shortcomings, but he was sticking with me, come hell or high water. A man of his word and a man of the Bible, Jay knew he lacked biblical grounds to divorce me.

Shortly before our wedding, Jay took me to a program at a very traditionally appointed church with beautiful stained-glass windows, wooden pews, hymnals, an elevated pulpit, and an eloquent, silver-haired pastor. The music was contemporary and the drama presentation was moving. At the end of the program, the sparkly-eyed pastor stood. "Has anyone here tonight felt the glory of the Lord fall on them?"

I looked around. The program had moved me to tears, but then I cry at high school pep rallies and every time I hear the national anthem.

"The glory of God is in this place! God has sent his Spirit here to save you because he loves you so much! All of us on this earth are sinners. The wages of sin is death, and that means we're all bound for eternal damnation unless we confess our sins to God Almighty and turn away from them. God the Father sent his Son, Jesus, to pay for all your sins! Jesus died in your place, and my place, and then rose from the dead after three days in the grave to prove he had conquered death. Jesus is the only way to God in heaven. Tonight, it's my prayer that anyone who has not already done so receive Jesus as their personal Savior. Do you feel the presence of the Lord? Invite him to save you!"

Actually, I *had* felt some kind of tug on my heart. I knew *for sure* I was a sinner. And I was pretty convinced there was a God. I knew Jesus was really important to Jay. I admired Jay's confidence for daily living, which he attributed to his faith in Christ. I wanted the assurance that I wouldn't burn in hell.

The silver-haired preacher said, "Pray with me, you who know you need saving."

Whatever "saved" meant, I knew I needed it, so I silently repeated the prayer after the pastor:

"Dear Jesus, I admit that I am a sinner ... Thank you for dying on the cross for my sins ... I am asking you to forgive me ... I open the door of my life and receive you as my Savior and Lord ... Thank you for giving me eternal life ... Amen."

After the prayer, the pastor said, "Now, if you just said that prayer for the first time, raise your hand and be counted among the new believers in Christ! We have a special gift for you."

I opened my eyes and looked around. Several people had their hands in the air. Ushers were moving in the aisles with booklets. I didn't raise my hand or collect the prize book and the congratulations the others got. I wanted to talk to Jay about it first.

When we got into the car to go home, he was quiet.

"That program about Jesus," I said, "it was so real. I prayed that prayer with the minister, the one about accepting Jesus as my Savior."

"I knew it!" he said. "I mean, I thought so. I hoped so. I saw you crying, and I just knew the Spirit was moving in you."

"Well, I don't know about a Spirit movement, but something made me think, *Well, I want to say that prayer.* But I wanted to tell you about it first. I'm still not sure if I did it right."

"I'll pray with you right now, just to be sure. Would you like that?"

The thought of saying it out loud, even with just the two of us in the car, made me uneasy. "I'll try," I said.

Jay led me through the whole thing again. Admitting my sin, asking for forgiveness, believing Jesus rose from the dead, and asking him to be my Savior. It was hard to choke the words out. I'd never thought I needed a God, because I had made myself a little throne of my own. But it felt good to move over enough to let God sit beside me.

When we said amen, Jay laughed and he whooped. He was so happy he spun doughnuts in the parking lot like a redneck who has been sampling his own moonshine.

It's too bad no one explained to me then that Jesus wants to be more than get-out-of-hell insurance, but that's all I knew. My pronouncement meant that Jay could stop feeling the weight of his mother's disapproval for marrying "outside the faith." In the run-up to our wedding, he had made all the wedding plans and preparations in the hope that I would make some sort of declaration of faith before the ceremony. So excited was he that I wasn't going to burn for eternity that he didn't pressure me to make any lifestyle changes afterward that might have helped us live more compatibly. Jay mistakenly thought that once I accepted Christ, a process of transformation would automatically begin. Somehow I would begin to supernaturally morph into a woman of wisdom, generosity, and loving-kindness. But lacking any spiritual guidance (or a personality transplant), my behavior remained constant. We were in for some long, cold, silent days, and some loud, throw-down shouting matches.

About four years into the marriage, Jay came home with a big announcement: "I met with the pastor today."

It didn't surprise me that I had been left out of that conversation. Marriage counseling had never been an option. Jay wouldn't have it. I thought, *Here it comes. He has figured out a way to send me packing.*

"I've decided to get rid of Ziggy," he said. "I called my mom and asked her if she would take him."

I didn't want to get my hopes up. Maybe I'd misheard. This was a huge peace offering if it wasn't a trap. "Take Ziggy where?"

"To live with my folks. In Wisconsin," he added, to make sure I understood.

"I don't know what to say," I said. It wasn't that I didn't *want* to say something. It's just that I didn't want to step on a land mine. Our house wasn't peaceful all that often. The last thing I wanted to do was mess it up.

"While I met with the pastor today," he went on, "I realized I haven't been the kind of husband I promised you I would be. I'm sorry."

I paused a long time, then ventured cautiously. "I haven't exactly been the wife of your dreams, either."

"I'd like to start over."

"I'd really like that too." No sarcasm. No positioning. No manipulation.

Oh, we'd had similar conversations. But they had never included Jay's willingness to get rid of his devil dog. There had always been remorse for hurtful barbs and insensitive behavior, and we would have peace in the house for a time. But we had never found a harmony that lasted very long.

This was different. This peace offering started something big. Something wonderful. Afterward, there were fewer and fewer tidal outbursts from either of us. Interestingly, the less Jay required me to change, the more I was willing to offer to him. I don't know if it was God or if we were so worn-down and worn-out that it had become easier to be quiet than to battle. Maybe all of the above—maybe God used our fatigue to guide our way to marital unity.

The old lady of the Lion Head Estate died. I finagled a look inside. The flawlessness of the place was depressing. It didn't look like anyone had ever lived in the house. There were no nicks in the doorjambs from little kids banging into them with a trike or a sword. The kitchen was pristine—no signs of family meals. The main-floor rooms were dark-wood paneled and oppressive. There was no evidence of play, of crazy fun—no evidence of life at all. It could have as easily been a museum display. How sad that I'd spent time envying that!

Jay and I finished renovating our little house across from the estate. I sat on my front porch contentedly admiring the view—now without wishing my life included it.

After lo those many years of battle, Jay and I were finally working together to redesign not just our house but our marriage. By the time the renovations were finished, I couldn't imagine life without him. I loved that man more than I had ever loved anyone outside my immediate family, and I trusted him completely. I told him my triumphant victories and catastrophic defeats before I told my mom. My heart was finally open to him, and I wanted more.

I wanted a baby. I wanted *his* baby.

We went into reproductive mode. I stopped taking the birth control pills I had been on for seventeen years.

It never occurred to me that I wouldn't get pregnant right out of the gate. Months passed and no pregnancy. Doctors couldn't find anything physically wrong with either of us, so we all assumed that birth control pills had stunted my baby-making abilities.

After almost a year of nonchalant, haphazard attempts with disappointing results, we got more focused: charting menstrual cycles, graphing body temperatures to determine optimum breeding conditions, deliberately refraining from sex in order to store up more sperm and encourage an eager flight to their waiting egg-y recipient. When all else failed, we became calculatingly reckless, resorting to unromantic sex night after night. *Just do it!* took on a personal but not endearing mantra for us, one probably never foreseen by a sneaker manufacturer.

We finally gave up on the idea of making our own children, and we rejected the idea of acquiring someone else's. Kids just weren't in the picture for us, we concluded, in spite of our heroic efforts to reproduce, plaintive pleas from Jay's mama, and persistent inquiries from my mom.

To take my mind off our failure, Jay decided to buy us a bigger house. He wanted another project home, but bigger and with more "character." We looked at farmhouses and Victorians, dilapidated dumps and places that looked like they should be on magazine covers. We settled on an old fixer-upper farmhouse sitting on nearly an acre, minutes from downtown

Grand Rapids. It seemed like a good compromise. he wanted to live on a big country lot, twenty minutes from a gallon of milk, and I wanted to live downtown in a gingerbread-trimmed Victorian.

We were one of seventy-five couples to go through that farmhouse in Western Michigan's very hot real-estate market. Having lost out on a couple of homes to quicker bidders, Jay decided to make an offer on this one before we even went through it—mostly because of the lot. It was the biggest house on the block, sitting majestically on that huge lawn. It was a fine home, one that Jay could picture in all its finished glory.

I was not so visually gifted.

Our bid was accepted. The house had been owned for the preceding thirty five years by a retired Catholic schoolteacher and his wife. Empty nesters, they were selling before any of their nine offspring decided to move back home. As you can imagine, with nine children there hadn't been much money for repairs, but there had been plenty of need for them, and the once-grand home was in need of a ton of repairs. Restoring it would take most of our discretionary income. We planned to support the local economy by paying someone else to do all the remodeling work we were fully capable of doing again but not at all interested in repeating so soon.

Jay was full of remodeling ideas—exciting, expensive ideas. The neighbors, who had feared that a developer would purchase the property and carve it up into rental units, sighed with relief when we introduced ourselves and our plans for the property.

We discovered I was pregnant twelve days after we signed the loan that had been approved based on our dual income.

Chapter 7

PREGNANT AND CONFOUNDED

Somehow I thought I would intuitively know when I was pregnant. A radiant glow would emanate from within. Surely pregnancy tests served merely to verify what a good mother already knew.

On the morning of my perfunctory monthly pregnancy test, I looked in the mirror. I wasn't radiating any glow, so I handed Jay the test stick I had just piddled on and told him he could babysit it for its ten-minute incubation period while I got ready for work. I wasn't expecting much—we'd been trying to reproduce for a long time, and so far I had failed to coax a single stick to turn pink for positive.

When he came into the bathroom while I was applying my mask du jour, his expression was deadpan. "Negative again, right?" I said.

He broke immediately into a proud grin. "Nope. We're pregnant!" he shouted, grabbing me around the waist and spinning me.

Funny. I didn't *feel* pregnant. But as soon as I knew I was, I started craving chow mein noodles and hot dogs.

To be honest, I didn't mind being pregnant. It was easy, once I got used to the morning queasiness, afternoon fatigue, and evening flatulence. I was peeing every ten minutes and my hormones were raging. I cried over sappy TV commercials and John Wayne movies. My body swelled into three giant bubbles, two in the front that looked like a fancy 3 and one lower in the rear for counterbalance. The worst part about being pregnant and not being able to see "down there" was accidentally putting my panty liners in sticky side up.

We referred to the protrusion in my belly as Binky, and I knew that if we didn't come up with some alternatives soon, it would stick. My grandma Hook had started calling my dad Tubby as a runt and it stuck with him for life. When I introduce my father to new friends as Tubby, they always look at me as if they're waiting for the punch line.

I wanted a name that was unique but not peculiar, distinctive but not weird. Something phonetic, two syllables max. With a last name like Andraszczyk, it would have to be concise. I came up with what I thought was the perfect name. "His name is Quimby," I announced to Jay, who promptly vetoed it with the same look on his face you get when you smell something foul. I was appalled—not because his reaction was so visceral, but because he wanted a vote! I thought he'd be so grateful that I had decided to have his children at all that he would let me name them. We would all have his last name—why couldn't I choose the first name?

When it became clear that Jay would be sharing naming privileges, we bought a book of baby names and started narrowing the options. Everyone in our circle of friends and acquaintances, even strangers at grocery stores, felt compelled to offer an opinion. I was flabbergasted by their responses to the names we were considering:

"I had a dog by that name, and he was the stupidest beast that ever lived."

"The meanest person I ever knew had that same name."

"I went to school with a girl named that. She was the ugliest girl in our school district."

"He'll be a sissy with a name like that!"

My personal favorite response: "Oh … is that a family name?"

We named our son Jacob. He was named for a great hero, but not of the Bible—of Hollywood. My husband and his whole family were avid John Wayne fans, and Jake, Big Jake, and Jacob are recurring names in his movies.

⌒∾⌒

Toward the end of my pregnancy, I became increasingly anxious. I had seen enough movies to know that women die giving birth. I was thirty-two, and at some point during every visit, the doctor said, "Well, you know, at your age …" My apprehension built until I made Jay promise that, if he had to make a choice between saving me or saving the baby, he would choose me. "We can have more children, but I'm irreplaceable," I reminded him.

My mom tried to reassure me by telling me that, in her experience, labor pains were really no worse than menstrual cramps, which neither of us had ever had. I hoped the genetics that had eased her labors had transferred to me.

She was the first person I called after Jake was born: "We had the baby tonight, he's perfect—*and you lied about the labor pains!*"

"What was I supposed to tell you? That it's like pulling a bowling ball through a nostril? What comfort would that be?"

Lying to mitigate fears seemed very reasonable to my mother, who was an accomplished storyteller.

Jay was the perfect partner for the delivery. As Jake slipped into the world, Jay was there to catch him, never taking his eyes off that boy until Jake was properly labeled as his progeny. Jake was born at 9:18 p.m., so by the time Jay left the hospital to head home, it was very late. He was still running on the adrenaline of witnessing a miracle but had no one to slap on the back, high five, or dump a barrel of Gatorade on. On his way home, he flagged down a policeman. "I just had to tell someone in person that I had a son today." The officer, a father himself, got out of his car to heartily congratulate Jay, pumping Jay's hand with both of his, then pounding him on the back.

Jay returned to the hospital the next day with dozens of roses, a box of blue, cigar-shaped bubble gum, and a smile that wouldn't quit. To bring Jake and me home from the hospital, he hired a limousine and filled it with balloons. I tried to enjoy the extravagance, listening to the driver as he pointed out landmarks and expounded on the historical buildings we passed on our tour, hoping the drugs would kick in and my fault line (as I affectionately referred to the episiotomy) would stop throbbing. My nipples were sore, and I wondered if I had missed an important chapter on nursing in all those books I'd read. The first time my milk "let down," I thought my breasts were melting. It felt like they were filling with water that's too hot, like when you step into a bathtub of scalding water without checking the temperature first.

I hadn't anticipated the physical effects of having a baby. What happened to my body? After the delivery, I fit completely inside my bath towel again, but what was all that gelatinous mush in my midsection? When I was pregnant, I was huge—but I was firm! After the delivery, my bladder was no longer the size of a peanut, but I had hemorrhoids the size of Michigan blueberries. After the delivery, I could hug anyone again. When I was pregnant, my body only nestled properly with skinny, big-bosomed women.

We had only been living in the farmhouse for about six months when we brought Jake home. The decision to quit my job and stay home with our baby meant that all the renovations we were planning to pay someone else to do either would not get done right away or we would have to do them ourselves. Not only had we sacrificed my income, but soon after Jake was born, Jay's company completely restructured his compensation package, slashing his income by half. He took a part-time job as a courier to make up some of the difference.

We were in a big house that needed lots of repairs with not much income and a new baby, and we were happy. It was a good time to be broke. We cut coupons. I made all of Jake's clothes, many of them from Jay's castoffs. We never went on vacation, and we rarely ate in restaurants. As most married couples will, we divided the workload. I took care of the baby and the home. Jay took care of the bills, the cars, the yard, anything that required a tool not sold in the housewares section, and anything that was dirty, heavy, or smelled bad.

Before Jake, Jay and I had unrealistic expectations for our children. They would never have dirty faces or clothes. They would adhere to the schedule we established. They would eat everything without complaint. They would never be sick. To that end, we set some parameters on behavior they would and wouldn't be exposed to. We would never leave them with babysitters, we would never swear in front of them, and we would never smoke in front of them.

That last one must have made God in heaven blow angel food out his nose. I liked everything about smoking: handling the cigarette, the ignition of matches and lighters, the pattern the flame burns into the butt, the dramatic inhaling and exhaling during conversations that hold a listener in suspense, the curling columns of smoke. Smoking regulated my weight and my bowel movements. It kept me company in the car, on the phone, and after meals like a conversation with a friend. I had smoked throughout the pregnancy—less than usual, but I had refused to give it up entirely. I knew smoking was hazardous to my own health and the health of our baby, but I didn't quit. I read about the side effects: premature births, low birth-weight babies, reduced oxygen levels that could cause brain damage, and the risk of heavy bleeding at delivery. I calculated the risk and kept lighting up.

Our decision to not smoke in front of the newborn child was the perfect opportunity for "Jehovah Sneaky" to get me to quit. He knew babies take up more time than I could ever have imagined, and that given the choice between sleeping and smoking, sleeping would win every time. If there were an Olympic event in sleeping, I would be a gold medalist. I have slept through alarms and phone calls. I once slept through the house getting hit by lightning.

There was no smoking in the hospital, but the change of routine and brevity of the stay made not smoking a non-issue. By the time we got home, I already had three days of not smoking behind me. My parenting inexperience, coupled with my reluctance to let Jake out of my sight, appreciably decreased my smoking opportunities. A thought crossed my mind: *Maybe I should quit.* I didn't say it out loud—God forbid I make myself accountable. But five days into it, I decided to see how long I could make it without smoking. Weeks piled up, triggers to reach for cigarettes subsided, and after six months I officially declared that I had quit smoking. It took another year before all the cravings stopped. I never picked it up again. Although when I delivered baby number two at 9 lbs. 14 oz., I was thinking that lower-birth-weight side effect might not be so bad.

I hadn't done a lot of babysitting when I was younger—no mother in her right mind wanted me watching her brood. So I had little experience with babies, much less with parenting. My mom's style of parenting had been to instill a value system and then let you try the variables. She used to say, "If you can read, you can learn anything," so I read volumes about how to grow a fertilized egg into a healthy baby and how to deliver that baby into the waiting hands of competent medical professionals. Not until I was about eight-and-a-half months pregnant did I start to read what to do with babies once you're no longer supervised by a team of experts. I'm more of a scholar than a clinician; I look great on paper, tests are a breeze, but practical application is my Achilles heel.

The first night home, I had to call the hospital to ask when to take Jacob out of the car seat. He looked so comfy in there, I thought maybe he'd be safest if I let him stay put and took him out only for feeding and changing. They said he'd be better in the drawer we had fixed up for him to sleep in. Actually, they didn't know it was a drawer. I made it sound like it was really a bassinet, something we didn't purchase until later.

We were blissfully ignorant as parents, unaware of the dangers to our child that lurked at every decision. He slept on his tummy and sucked his thumb. Jay's mom insisted that all her babies had been potty trained by six months old, but we kept Jacob in diapers until he was three years old and lived with the shame. I would have used disposable diapers, because I had a high tolerance for guilt, but again, finances being what they were, we used cloth and I washed them at home.

I was inundated with advice about everything. One camp insisted that scheduling a newborn's feeding and sleeping schedules would make a happy home. I decided I would never wake a sleeping baby and we would all eat when we were hungry, or bored, or the food looked irresistible. Jake's first food was chocolate, a Kit Kat bar to be exact, which Jay shared with him because it was, in fact, irresistible. I nursed him because the doctor said it was the best choice for him, but also because it was easier in the middle of the night and because it was the first time in my life that I'd filled out a sweater like a 1950s movie star.

Time turns elastic in the fog of sleep deprivation. I was folding clothes at midnight and still in jammies and ponytail at two in the afternoon. Not a problem—I loved my rubberized clock. Being Jay's wife and Jacob's mommy was the best. I was born for this! I loved my husband for not giving up on me. For giving me the option of staying home full-time with my baby. I loved that he had moved his office home to be with me, even if he wasn't really available. Used to having a demanding job, I was unaccustomed to having downtime during the day, so when Jake napped, I would wander into Jay's office to tell him some random tidbit gleaned from a phone conversation or to ask, "Whatcha doin'?" He finally explained that while he was working, even though he was home, he was unavailable to me for anything short of an emergency. He was accessible only for capital Jake moments, like the first smile, the first bite of solid food, the first step.

Jacob was my responsibility and I was Jay's. He worked hard so that I could stay home, but with that bit of respite came all the responsibility of the baby, including every nighttime feeding and messy diaper. Being such an accomplished sleeper, I fretted that I wouldn't hear Jake during the night, so at first we kept him in our bedroom. Not a great solution—all his snorting and cooing and breathing kept me on such high alert that I never got any rest. I had also read somewhere that even tiny babies can be traumatized if they witness violent acts, such as a man making passionate love to a woman. So when I got the nod from the doctor that my fault line was shored up and secure, I was reluctant to subject our newborn child to the trauma of his parents "being together," as married couples do.

Jay's solution? He unceremoniously moved Jake into an adjacent room. "Buy a baby monitor!" Pecking order established, everyone got what they needed, and we all were better for it.

⁓

Before long, I didn't even need the baby monitor to tell me when Jake was up, wet, crying, or hungry. My body recuperated quickly, even at my age, and rocking Jake, late in the night after a feeding, I was overwhelmed by my good fortune. Jake's head was on my shoulder, he was dry, fed, and burped, well on his way to sleep. I had one hand on his perfectly shaped head and the other supporting his little bottom. Moonlight was cascading through the bedroom window, refracting off the snow and lighting the warm room in the quiet house. *How does a woman like me end up here?* I wondered. *How did my life get so good? I have a husband who loves me, a fine house, and a healthy baby boy.*

It was exactly then that I heard the voice of God and he said, "Robyn, what are you going to tell your son about me?" The masculine voice spoke gently but with complete authority. There was no condemnation, but there was a question—and an answer was required.

I stopped rocking. I didn't *know* what I was going to tell my son about God—because I didn't know much. What if Jake asked questions about God when Jay wasn't home? I didn't want to look stupid to my boy. Despite Jay's imperfections and his unhealthy addictions, he had been raised in a Christian home, he knew Jesus, he read his Bible. The only time I called on the name of Jesus Christ was if I stubbed my toe or if I was so furious with Jay that I wanted someone or something bigger than me to smite him.

I know what to do if I want to learn something new. Either buy a book or take a class. I opted to take a class so I could follow the lead of some God guru to the answers I would need for Jake's questions and God's inquiry.

I called Jay's church, the one I pretended to attend when his parents visited, and told them I was looking for some information about God so when our son asked questions I wouldn't sound like an idiot. The nice lady on the phone thought I might do well in a Bible study. The church offered one for ladies on Tuesday mornings, complete with child care for Jake. That sounded good to me—there was probably a lot of stuff about God in the Bible. So I signed up for it over the phone. That the church called it a *Ladies'* Bible Study prickled me to no end, since the study designed for males was for *men*, but the female's study was for *ladies*. I had been trained to interpret this as an obvious slur implying the inferiority of women. But I was desperate. I had taken a peek at Jay's Bible and knew I would need assistance. It was such a big book, and I didn't want to waste time on the unnecessary or uninteresting parts; the Bible study, I assumed, would focus on the most relevant parts of the Bible. There was no cost for the class, and the child care fee was negligible—a good thing, since in our home discretionary income was a faint memory.

"What will I need to bring?" I asked the woman.

"Just a pencil and a Bible," she said. "All the curriculum is provided."

I was so pleased with myself. That night at dinner I said, "Guess what I did today?"

"I don't know, honey—what did you do?

"I signed up for a Bible study at your church."

On the outside, Jay was calm and collected as he said, "Isn't that wonderful!" On the inside, I'm sure he was doing the happy dance of all happy dances.

"I need a Bible," I said, "and I don't want to use yours because you've ruined it. It's all marked up. Besides, I looked at it and it's full of *thees* and *thous*. Do you have one in American English?" Bless his heart and his ability to keep a poker face; he kept his composure and told me I should take $20.00 to the Christian bookstore and pick out a new Bible for myself.

"You Christians have your own bookstores?" I said incredulously.

Jake and I ventured to the Christian bookstore the next day. I proudly told the counter clerk that I was signed up to take a Bible class and that I would be needing a Bible. I thought my request was an extraordinary one; I had no idea how many people go into Christian bookstores every day with similar requests. The clerk pointed me to the Bible section, and as I walked toward it I wondered why they needed a whole section just for the Bible—how many different color covers can there be? I found not just varieties of covers—soft, hard, leather, and so on—but many different versions! Who knew the same book could be written in different versions? Not I! Is that even legal? King James, New King James, New

Living, NIV, NASB, ESV, red letter, Bibles with commentaries, Bibles with things called devotionals. There were specific Bibles for women, for men, for students, for teens, and for children. There were study Bibles and vocational Bibles. I picked up an impressive-looking Bible, but the price made me put it down so fast that onlookers might have thought it was on fire. They cost the earth!

I went back to the counter a bit more humbly and pleaded for help. I explained that I had $20.00 and that I liked pink and mentioned the name of the church where I was taking my class. She found me a plain black Bible in my price range, with big print and wide margins. She pointed out that this meant I could write notes around the printed text. It had a table of contents, some colorful maps, and a concordance, which was apparently some kind of study reference. The sales clerk thought it was very important that I have one with a concordance.

Armed with my new Bible, a fine-point pen, and a yellow highlighter, off to class I went. I would love to tell you it was wonderful, but it wasn't.

I did not fit in.

The women in the group looked like they belonged in magazines. Their hair was done and their cars were clean. Their clothes were dry clean only, and those who wore jeans had sharp creases pressed into them. Nobody else ever slipped and cussed. None of them consulted the table of contents to find Proverbs, and they all knew John the Baptist didn't write any of the chapters titled John. Except they didn't call them chapters—they were *books*. (The Bible, it turns out, is a collection of sixty-six books bound together in one big book. Who knew?) The women in the group knew there was a Joseph in the Old Testament and *another* Joseph in the New Testament. Both Josephs are principle figures, but in entirely different stories! Who could keep all this stuff straight? They kept telling me how creative God was—well, couldn't God come up with unique names for the key players?

I was very confused. Each week we were given homework assignments to prepare us for the lesson. I tried to do my homework; I laboriously looked up the Bible reference in the table of contents, found the page, chapter and verse, read it, read the question again, reread the verse— but it rarely made sense to me. I would get so aggravated that I'd hurl my Bible across the floor, sending it scooting across the floor and smacking the wall. I would scratch big question marks all over my homework in frustration and highlight chunks of the lesson for further discussion in class.

I challenged everyone.

I questioned everything.

"Where did you get that answer?"

"How do you know that's what the author meant?"

"Why is that important?"

Weeks into the class, Louise, one of the women in the group, called me at home. She was a sweet thing, maybe ten or fifteen years older than me, with teenaged children and a Southern accent. Those Southern women intimidate me—they're so cordial and calm. "Robyn, honey," she said, as if my name was now four syllables long, "are you having any trouble with the Bible lessons?" She elongated the first syllable of Bible until it sounded more like a short *A* than a long *I*.

I ignored her slaughter of my mother's English language and admitted that I was, indeed, having trouble with the Bible lessons. "I have always been a good student," I whined, "but I'm having problems assimilating and regurgitating this stuff. How can a text that's been made into a comic book be so perplexing?"

She was entirely sympathetic—no big surprise, being Southern and all. "Well, I've been thinking about that," she drawled, "and I was wondering if it would be okay with you if I came over to your house every week while your baby naps and do the lesson with you—to help prepare you for the class."

"That would make you my new best friend," I said.

Louise tutored me through the whole year. She checked my homework and answered all the additional questions I had scrawled in the margins. She brought me resource materials that clarified and illuminated cultural references and historical relevance. And she helped me understand that the women I thought were perfect and polished weren't perfect at all—but their God was!

Through Louise's indulgent tutoring and the remarkable teaching from Helen, the bossy lecturer who always seemed to be pointing her long finger right at me, I realized I needed more than answers for Jake, or even get-out-of-hell insurance for myself.

I learned there is a God in heaven who loves me. Not a chintzy little "luv ya," either, like when you're trying to get off the phone. *Okay, I gotta go now, love ya, bye-bye.* And not an "I know about you and I choose to love you because I am supposed to" love you. This God in heaven, God the Father, loves me because he made me. He knows all about me and he loves me right where I am and as I am. Sure, he's hoping for more for me—a better life, a healthier life, an easier life, if I will just make wiser choices—but God loves me just as I am and he always has! Who wouldn't want to spend time basking in that love? I did!

The thing that prevented me from wallowing and rolling in God's love for me was my own sin. God is perfect and holy—he can't tolerate sin; he can't abide it or have sin in his presence. Not even one sin. Not even a little bitty sin. There's *no* sin in God's presence. I knew I had sinned, and I knew there was no hope of a cosmic balance sheet where my good stuff outweighed my bad. The only way for a sinful person like me—or anyone else—to have access to the Holy God is by accepting Jesus Christ's death as a complete payment for all my sins and his resurrection as the final victory over death. To have a relationship with God the Father, I needed to receive his Son, Jesus Christ, as my Lord and Savior, so the Spirit of God could dwell in me. I could have access to God the Father's heart and ear through Jesus. I could have a fresh start. I could choose to be a new creation.

Saying that I acknowledged Jesus as Savior, as I had at the church program before Jay and I married, secured my eternal life in heaven after death. What I hadn't known then was that my confession of faith in Jesus Christ had also secured my life *until* death. I didn't have to wait to die to experience God!

I had heard the names Holy Spirit and Holy Ghost but didn't really understand who that was. In the months following my surrender to Jesus, not just as Savior but as King, as Lord, I began to understand that there's a third part to God, and that part's job is to teach me about Jesus and to convict me of sin (a full-time job in itself). The Holy Spirit began to coach me, inspire me, send up danger flares, and yes, even speak to me. Sometimes God spoke to me like a thought traipsing across the backyard of my mind. Other times it would be in the lyrics of a song, or a verse in my Bible, or a portion of a sermon on the radio or from the pulpit.

It happened all the time.

I would never call God annoying, but persistent? Definitely! Thoughts of correction and confession would "occur" to me:

Use a kinder tone of voice.

Think of others first.

Say you're sorry.

Send a thank-you card.

Quit flirting with other men.

Fix dinner.

Stay on your budget.

I must admit the more obedient I was, the more compliant I was with God's instructions, the faster I did what he said to do when he said to do it, the better my life worked. This was great! There was immediate blessing for obedience. Not always financial blessing, but harmony in my home, satisfaction in my work, contentment with our house, my hair, clothes, kids, car, and so on.

As a woman who understood how much I was loved by God, the desires of sin had less allure. I didn't need sin to make me feel good, because I *already* felt good—as a recipient of God's love for me.

I stayed in that Bible study for years. I became a group leader, then a teacher. I kept reading my Bible and praying for wisdom. Even as a leader, I continued to ask women more mature in the faith than I was to tutor me. Women beginning their spiritual journey began calling my house seeking advice! My husband was so proud of me and so pleased with me. I was calmer and more patient—actually pleasant to live with. Our clashes were few, and Jay and I worked to solve problems rather than to win battles.

By the time Jake was two, I was in a groove. Jake was a good baby turned toddler. He ate everything, slept twelve hours at night, and took naps in the afternoon. He traveled well and rarely fussed about anything. He had a long attention span and a growing monosyllabic vocabulary. He could identify and name letters of the alphabet out of sequence and was starting to do simple addition. He loved running around in a diaper, a policeman's hat, and cowboy boots. He didn't like to be sticky, and when we played with homemade playdough, he would say, "You do it, Mama." He drew with pencils, but didn't like the feel of crayons. He had a creative imagination. I could structure his schedule, which meant I still had control of mine. He was happy and funny, and that made Jay and me happy too. If one child is this good, why not have another?

The pregnancy with the second baby was perfectly textbook. Although the phrase "at your age" was again part of every doctor's appointment and every conversation with my grandma, I liked being pregnant. I probably could have done it for a living had we been able to part with the babies. Surrogate mothers were all over the news, and I thought, *How hard could that be?* But Jay said, "No way," so I let go of the idea of being someone else's garden.

Eli's birth was not the calm flow of events that Jake's was. Labor started in the middle of the night, not at 9:00 a.m., so I was short on rest. He was nose up instead of down, and he was not interested in departing the womb. We battled for sixteen hours—I would push and he would wiggle right back up the birth canal. Finally his head crowned, and the team of doctors suctioned a mini plunger to it and hauled him out screaming. I can't blame him; it was the worst thing that had happened to him in his whole life.

The drama of Jake's birth was discovering at his quiet entrance that he had his umbilical cord wrapped around his neck four times so that he came out looking a bit purple. Eli's head was egg shaped from the plunger apparatus. "He's not going to stay like that, is he?" was my first question. Assured that it wasn't permanent, I collapsed back onto the table. Having a baby takes a lot out of you, if you'll pardon the pun.

Eli went from the doctor's catch to Jay's waiting arms, where he was welcomed into the world by a man whose capacity for love knew no bounds. We wondered if we could love the second child as much as the first, but in the nanosecond it takes to memorize his squishy face, God multiplied our hearts and the question seemed absurd. Jay never let Eli out of his grasp until the bracelets were affixed and the genealogical association was established.

Both Jake and Eli had Jay's body, though Jake was blond with blue eyes and Eli came with a head of black hair and eyes that turned a deep brown over the next six months. Like Jake, Eli got the royal treatment for his hospital departure: limo (with a different driver this time—no unnecessary tour narration), roses, more colorful balloons. Eli was an easier baby than Jake, but only because by the time he came home with me I knew I didn't have to keep him next to me 24/7. I could be sure he'd be safe in a playpen for the two minutes it took to check a pot on the stove or flip the wet clothes into the dryer.

Even though Eli was an easy infant, having two children tanked my schedule. Jake was three when Eli came home. He had been potty trained and was sleeping in a big-boy bed. He was done with naps but still took a quiet time mid-afternoon, playing independently with toys or looking at books. Eli never needed as much sleep as the rest of us. He hated missing out on visitors or meals. We joked that the sound of chewing was like an alarm clock for him. No one even chewed gum in the house if Eli was sleeping!

There isn't much that's flexible about me. I hate change—unless it's my idea. My spices are alphabetized, my closet is color coded and arranged by sleeve length. All the coins in my car are heads up, facing the windshield! One child I could bully into keeping order, especially one like Jake who thrived on routines. But the structure I had maintained with one child disappeared with two. They never slept at the same time. I'm sure they formed a conspiracy early on: "Okay, I'm really tuckered out, so you'll have to get Mom up tonight."

If the baby sleeps through the night, the toddler will wet the bed or have a bad dream. If you take them grocery shopping, one will insist on walking, which slows you down so that the other one can decide he's starving halfway through. You either watch your ice cream melt in the cart as you nurse or leave the grocery store to return at midnight to finish the task. The stroller your toddler has refused to use since last year will be reclaimed as soon as you try to put the baby in it. That goes for every rattle, stuffed animal, and blanket in the house. Even if you manage to have same-sex children and think you'll save money on clothes, they will be out of season for the size you need by the time you try to use them.

For the first months of Eli's life, I thought it took having two children for me to discover I should have had only one. I was cranky and frustrated with the lack of control and my messy house. This became the subject of many discussions with other new moms. Mentoring moms would gently say, "Time goes so fast! They'll be grown before you know it. Just enjoy the time with them." I tried, but I just wasn't getting what I wanted done, done! My to-do list was getting longer and longer.

I devised a plan that allowed me to clean the entire house every week, breaking the chore list up by days, breaking up projects so they could be completed during nap time. One afternoon, Eli just didn't want a nap. He played on the kitchen floor while I chopped and prepped dinner, then wiped down counters and appliances. Finally there was only one chore left on the list for that day: mopping the kitchen floor.

I ran the water and moved Eli into the next room to play, but he kept crawling back into the kitchen. After several trips, he was so wet I decided to simply mop around him.

I turned my back to him—just for a moment—to rinse the mop. In no time at all, there was a loud crash, and I spun to see what had happened.

In the few seconds my back had been turned, Eli had pulled himself upright using the kitchen table leg. Moving around the edge of the table, he'd grabbed one of the legs of the heavy oak chairs I'd perched on top of the table while the floor was drying. Eli tugged, and the chair tipped over, falling on top of him, pinning him to the ground. There he lay on the floor, covered by the heavy chair. Still. Quiet.

"Oh my God!" I cried aloud. I was frozen in alarm.

In my spirit, I heard God say, "If this child is too much trouble for you, I can take him back."

"No, no, no!" I cried as I rushed to Eli. "I want him. I'm sorry."

As I scooped him up, he started howling. He'd just had the wind knocked out of him. There wasn't a cut, scrape, or bruise on him.

"Mama's so sorry, Eli. I love you. I love you."

I wish I could say that I never complained about my children interrupting my chore schedule or social calendar again, but that would be a lie. I did, but rarely. Sometimes I forgot how I had begged God for them—how fragile life is, and how quickly everything can change.

I loved every season with Jake and Eli. By the time they were six and three, Jay was comfortably working from home. He was on track to be Salesman of the Year. We had managed to freshen up some of the rooms in the house with paint and paper and Jay was nearly finished remodeling the kitchen. I had loads of friends, other moms with small children who came over to talk and play. The best part about having a house with ancient carpeting and ugly walls is that you don't freak out when it's full of toddlers holding crayons and cups of grape juice.

Both Jake and Eli were walking, talking, potty trained, and sleeping through the night. They ate when we ate and went to bed at 7:30 p.m. every night. They were interesting and creative and adorable. Jay and I were rested and appreciative of each other. It was still a bit lonely around the table at holidays, but my mom visited every six weeks or so and Jay's parents came over a lot too. Even our favorite football team, the Green Bay Packers, was having a great year.

It just doesn't get any better than this.

I bumped into Louise, the lovely Southern woman who had taken me on as her personal project that first year of Bible study. By then, I was teaching my own class and understood what a sacrifice it had been for her to haul all her materials across town every week and what a pain in the rear I had been with my worldly viewpoints and time-consuming questions. When I saw her, I nearly fell over myself trying to thank her for all she had done. I assured her that I had been good soil and that I was very fruity (showing off my spiritual vocabulary)—teaching Bible classes, facilitating large ministry events, speaking the Name of Jesus to women. I told her of my husband's pleasure with me. I was eager for her to know that I had not been a waste of her time.

She smiled at me the way the ladies from the South do, nodding affirmation, and said, "Well, shoot, Robyn, honey, I'm glad to hear all that, but, you know, you were taking up so much class time somebody had to do something with you, and I just drew the short straw!"

Chapter 8

THE GRAND SCHEME

We called it the Grand Scheme. Jay's parents' health was marginal. They lived in a house in Wisconsin that was falling down around their ears. Why not sell that place and build a brand-new home near us?

It seemed to me they were at my house all the time anyway. Why not move them to the area so they could go home at night? Since the arrival of Jake and Eli, on whom the moon was hung for Andy and Helen, they had been visiting more and more often. The fact that they brought both big Doberman pinschers along wasn't exactly a bonus feature. I secretly kept track of their unwelcome invasions by making angry red circles around those dates in my checkbook register. When they weren't at our house, it seemed Jay was at theirs—fixing a leaky roof, broken equipment, or a deteriorating outbuilding. The more often Jay went back to help them, the more obvious it became that it was only a matter of time before his parents would lose the battle against the property's maintenance demands.

It might not be so bad, I thought. They could babysit our little guys so Jay and I could try one of those date nights I kept hearing about at church. Holidays would certainly be more festive with grandparents in the mix, right? But even as we plotted the Grand Scheme my uncertainty rose. "They have *got* to live at least ten miles from us!" I said over and over to Jay. Just a little distance to keep them from being around all the time, like they were when we lived in Wisconsin. Jay agreed. He loved his parents, but he saw the merit in having some mileage between our homes.

Helen was a sweet woman of Irish/English descent with a strong Louisiana accent that made words like *oil* rhyme with *hole*, and who said, "Well I never," when I really knew she certainly would. She put the emphasis on odd syllables and called everyone but me *Hon*. She cooked everything on high and, surprisingly, the food mostly turned out well. She'd found Jesus in her thirties and read her Bible every morning and every night whether she felt like it or not.

Andy was a retired Milwaukee motorcycle cop with an unflattering opinion of most doctors, women in general, and minorities at large. He loved his wife and his kids, having big dogs, and eating gross amounts of food in front of others who would be both astonished and horrified. He once ate thirty-eight trout in front of a cheering audience of strangers at an all-you-can-eat diner. He bragged about riding American-made, Harley Davidson motorcycles year-round in the 1960s when he was on the police force—before they let women on patrol and everything was ruined. "Hell, yes, it was cold. We'd wrap our legs with newspaper as insulation under our uniforms during the winter months. Not like it is now—the department wasn't full of wimps and women." He bragged, "Helen polished my boots every night." What a dutiful wife. He recounted holiday parades he'd driven in and celebrities he had escorted.

On one of President Eisenhower's visits to Milwaukee, Andy rode as an escort. The president stopped his car and called to Andy, "Hey, soldier, don't I know you?"

Andy approached the car and suggested that maybe the general remembered meeting him in Germany. "I was the Army's undefeated heavyweight Golden Gloves boxing champion in 1945."

"Yes, yes, that's right. You were quite a showman!" Eisenhower said, chuckling as he vigorously shook hands with Andy before proceeding with the route.

Andy never missed an opportunity to tell about meeting Jay Silverheels, who played Tonto on *The Lone Ranger* television show. "He was the nicest Injun I ever met. That's why I named my son Jay," he said. I never bothered to mention that Tonto is Spanish for dummy; since he didn't name my husband Tonto it didn't seem relevant—although Dummy was a favorite moniker of his for anyone who displeased or perturbed him.

Andy assigned lots of pet names and nicknames. His wife, Helen, was Babe when she wasn't Dummy, and I was Skinny—not enough womanly padding on my frame for his taste. I'm not sure his dog Oscar ever knew his name, since Andy never called him anything but Sonofabitch, as in "Lay down, Sonofabitch." Even devout Helen, who would never curse, had to start calling him Sonofabitch, too, to get the dog to respond.

Andy and Helen had met in Germany toward the end of World War II. Andy was in the army and Helen was an army brat, the daughter of an army officer. She volunteered as a dance instructor for the USO. Andy took Helen out to eat and to USO dances; he invited her to come and watch him fight. She did once. Andy annihilated his opponent in the first round. Helen cried for two days and never went to another match. After they got married, Helen said she couldn't stand it that Andy boxed, so he gave it up, although during the early lean years on the police force, she tolerated Andy moonlighting as the Masked Marvel, a pro wrestler. Apparently, to Helen, wrestling was less dangerous than boxing and more like pugnacious gymnastics. She even made the masks he pulled over his head to protect his identity from the Milwaukee Police Department—to no avail, since at one event Andy's distinctive tattoos caught the police captain's eye. That ended his wrestling career.

There is no doubt that he was a powerful man. Andy and Helen were out on a date one evening and came upon a gang of "hopped-up mugs," as Andy called them. They made lewd remarks to Helen as they approached the couple. Andy put Helen behind him and warned the thugs away, but they weren't to be deterred. Andy told Helen to run. She ran about a block and then turned around to see all five would-be assailants on the ground and Andy rubbing his knuckles.

Andy loved to recount his glory days of high-speed motorcycle chases, several of which ended in bone-breaking crashes—so many, in fact, that he had to take early retirement from the Milwaukee PD on a disability pension. Later, he had two heart attacks. Andy wasn't the same after the second one. He changed from the attentive and loving husband who had wooed Helen in Germany into a cantankerously charismatic man, unhappy if there was no audience to witness his charm.

All of that happened before I knew him. By the time Andy entered my life, he exceeded his fighting weight by 150 pounds and our boys distinguished him from their other grandpa by referring to him as the grandpa with the big belly. They adored him. Grandpa-with-the-Big-Belly showered them with presents and treats they weren't supposed to have and woke them up early from naps they didn't want to take.

As Jay and I planned the Grand Scheme, getting Helen out of a house that was slowly killing her pocketbook and her happiness seemed like a decent trade-off for the disadvantages of moving Andy closer. Besides, I kept telling myself, he was in such terrible condition that it was merely a matter of time before he'd eat too much fried food, refuse to take his medication or follow the doctor's instructions, and die. Then Helen would be left with her low-maintenance cottage and have time to teach Bible studies, garden, paint, and go to garage sales anytime she wanted.

Jay and I talked with them often about the advantages of moving closer to us. Finally, Andy and Helen listed their home—a six-bedroom farmhouse with a large yard and several outbuildings, including a huge barn—for sale. Even in its dilapidated state, it sold three days later for full asking price and without additional inspections—to a lovely homosexual couple. And I can't even write what Andy thought of that!

Helping them pack to move, we waded through three decades of memories. Helen finally surrendered to the dumpster's yawn the ancient treasures of her children's grade school artwork, broken toys, and stuffed animals. She reluctantly gave up mismatched and outdated possessions and small appliances that hadn't worked for years. With each toss, the task became easier, until finally she had weeded out anything that wasn't genuinely valuable, truly sentimental, or necessary to their new life.

But that was just the house. The main floor of their barn was filled to the corners with tons of Andy's automotive tools, as well as furniture Helen had collected at antique stores and rummage sales. The second story of the barn housed Helen's once-thriving upholstery business, with heavy sewing machines and thousands of yards of fabric.

They built their new house on ten acres of land about a thirty-minute drive from us, added an enormous pole barn to house all of Andy's automotive tools, and invited Jay to keep his car projects in it. Clever! Enticing him to spend his free time at their house. Oh, I was welcome— as long as I brought those babies they loved so much.

Discarder's remorse hit Helen with another wave of tears as we unpacked them in Michigan. The new house was only a third the size of the old, and the fresh smell and pristine condition didn't assuage the loss of space and character they had in their old farmhouse.

Instead of looking at what wasn't, however, Helen focused on what was. She had more disposable income to spend, plus she could garden and shop and take my kids anytime she wanted—and she wanted them a lot. Is this heaven? Our plan was gelling perfectly. No more Thanksgiving dinners for four. No more vacations spent replacing roof shingles on someone else's house. The possibilities of a date night were looking good.

God must have missed the memo about the Grand Scheme because, POOF, Helen died of a heart attack in her front yard just months after they moved in. Even though she was overweight and had been experiencing shortness of breath, her death caught all of us by surprise. We had been so focused on our version of the Grand Scheme we didn't consider that God might have an alternate plan.

Jay was traumatized by his mama's death. The day she died, he watched the EMTs try to resuscitate her to no avail. I believe once she saw Jesus and the pearly gates of heaven, not even her favorite son's pleas to return could persuade her to come back to dwell in her broken-down body.

Her funeral was held at the tiny country church near their new home in Michigan. Friends and relatives from Wisconsin and Michigan came to console Andy. Craig, the childhood friend of Jay's who had flown him to see me at the Playboy Club at Lake Geneva, came for her funeral. Craig's dad, Willy, died when Craig was fourteen, and Andy had taken him out for burgers or movies or both every week until Craig graduated from high school and went off to Embry Riddle Aeronautical School. Craig and Jay talked about old times and the giant holes dead parents leave. I heard Craig tell Jay, in a moment of empathetic reflection, that his own life had ended the day his dad's plane crashed, and he was just spending the rest of his days waiting to join him—that he lived as a risk taker because the void his dad left couldn't be filled. It was both heartbreaking to hear and heartwarming to listen to as the two friends consoled each other.

That one moment of tenderness did not endear Craig to me. I couldn't decide if he was truly solicitous or setting the stage to tell another audacious story of his own. He had been married three times and was currently single—no surprise. "I'm terrific at weddings, but *sucked* at marriage," he joked. What a horrible word. "I've tried all the formulae: *He loves her, she loves him*—that didn't work. *He loves her, she hates him*—that didn't work. *He hates her, she loves him*—that didn't work either. The only one left to try is *she hates him, he hates her,* but I can't find anyone to try it with." He calculated that forever was approximately four years and three months long, based on the average length of his marriages.

He was so full of himself, going on at great length about his visits to exotic places, both tropical and desert. He had been to the four corners of the world and wasn't impressed: "I can enjoy the trees of Wisconsin as much as the trees in Europe, and the sands of Egypt looked a lot like the beaches of Lake Michigan, but hotter." He bragged of flouting danger, flying planes in all climates and weather, and making thousands of sky-dives. Asked about his piloting skills, he'd feign humility: "It's no big deal. Flying a plane is like being a bus driver."

What an attention junkie! He ate too much, talked too loudly, and monopolized conversations. I thought he was obnoxious.

There was, however, that streak of kindness and generosity in him. He knew Jay loved the Green Bay Packers, so one Sunday Craig flew to Grand Rapids, picked Jay up, and flew to Green Bay to sit in the hallowed seats of Lambeau Field and watch the Packers in person. After the wet but victorious game, the field's sod was torn up and big clumps of muddy grass were piled up in the end zone by the groundskeepers. Seizing a once-in-a-lifetime opportunity to capture a bit of sacred ground, Jay and Craig begged custodians for pieces of the sod to take home. Jay presented the soggy mud to me with such enthusiasm that I didn't have the heart to tell him I didn't want it in the house. He researched the best lighting, plant food, and base soil for his project. We planted it in a wash bucket, poked it full of plant food stakes, and parked it in front of a window, where it grew into a thick rectangle of lush Lambeau Field grass. Jay was thrilled. So was our cat. Grass is so effective for dislodging hairballs.

Helen's death tested everybody. Andy had depended on her to be his social-event planner, personal financier, companion, and friend— his absolution and his trophy. His faith was shallow. Although no one doubted his belief in Jesus as the Son of God and Savior of the world, he had always worshipped vicariously through Helen. He enjoyed the non-sanctuary aspects of church: the potlucks and special programs, being in charge of parking and security, and the restaurant gatherings after the service.

Jay's faith, on the other hand, was so deep that he had always felt like the chosen child, a favorite of his parents and of God. When the Grand Scheme failed, Jay became angry with God for taking his mom and leaving us to deal with the difficult Andy. He questioned where the justice was, for both Helen and himself. He wanted his mom back, and he certainly did not want to have to comfort the man he held responsible for the stress to her heart that led to her premature demise. He just couldn't accept that Helen was better off with her Jesus in heaven, because he wasn't better off without her on earth.

It did seem unfair. Without Helen to buffer family and strangers alike from Andy's behavior and outbursts, and with Jay in the throes of grieving, it fell entirely to me to take care of Andy. He came for supper every day—at ten in the morning! He stayed in my path all day. Suddenly, I was the one handing him his pills, catering to his eating preferences, and listening to his running diatribes about what was wrong with America.

Feeding him was an exercise in frustration. He wouldn't eat a casserole—he didn't like his food touching, much less all mixed up. He didn't eat any cheese, not even on pizza. He didn't even like the smell of it. He would say to the boys, "You aren't going to put stinky cheese (parmesan) on your spaghetti, are you?" He also wouldn't eat at anyone else's house—said he was suspicious of their housekeeping, although he would eat at the greasiest diners on the planet. Of course, he would eat anyone's desserts.

He would sit at our supper table telling off-color stories, using words I didn't want my toddlers to know. He chewed with his mouth open, ingesting massive wads of food, and still continued to poke forkfuls into his mouth. It was his way of either enjoying one of the remaining pleasures of life or committing slow suicide. It disgusted me.

He went everywhere the kids and I went—grocery stores, swimming pools, restaurants. What he couldn't flirt with, he fought with. He would poke and push around young men at McDonald's when he interpreted their behavior as fresh or disrespectful. When we passed drivers with coffee cups or cell phones in their hands, he would push as much of himself out the window as would fit, shake his fist, and yell at them.

The worst by far was when he would pat me on the backside and call me Baby.

I wondered how long it would be before either he died or my head exploded.

Right after Helen died, Andy joked that he didn't know why women complained about housekeeping because it certainly wasn't rocket science. "It's not like they have to drag the laundry to the river and beat the clothes on a rock. You just push buttons and the machines do all the work. Same for dishes and vacuuming." What do you expect from a man who had never lifted a dustpan?

One day, rather than showing up at our house long before noon as he usually did, he called to ask if the boys could come out to his house to play. At first I welcomed the break in routine—until I realized that it was just his way of revealing a mess too big for him to clean up without admitting he needed help. There were dishes molding in the sink, fourteen loads of sweaty, urine-dribbled clothes in a mound in the laundry room, science projects in the refrigerator, and what looked like fossils on the stovetop and in the microwave.

When it was all scraped, scoured, laundered, and tidied, Andy repeated the cycle—until I decided that having two households to manage was too much and we hired a cleaning company. That lasted about a month. Our account was dismissed, probably because Andy was tipping the young women with wine coolers, but the account rep just said they were too busy to retain us.

Jay's grief deepened. He smoked pot daily to mitigate the pain. To dull the pain in his side. The pain of losing his mom. The pain of life. He didn't smoke pot or cigarettes in front of the children, and since they had the full run of the house, that meant Jay spent a lot of time locked away in his home office or out in the garage. Away from us.

I asked him to quit. I prayed. I whined. I prayed. I reasoned. And I prayed some more. I even yelled a little. "It's illegal! What if you get busted? Do you think your company is going to be as understanding about a drug charge as they were about the DWI?" His use of pot continued unabated.

I worried about his breaking the law. About pot's effects on him and on our marriage. About what I should do about it. I never told a soul.

Most of the other moms with whom I exchanged play dates had grown up in church. I was always worried one of them would smell marijuana in the house or on the boys and report us to Child Protective Services, and that I would lose Jay to jail, my kids to the State, and my home to foreclosure.

Finally I gave up. It had become a part of our lives. I resolved to not make his drug use an issue in our home. I had made my position clear.

He wasn't going to quit, but he was as responsible with it as he could be with an illegal substance. He never drove high. He went to work and never got high there. He paid the bills on time and continued to maintain the cars and home as he always had. He didn't use in front of the boys. He didn't make drug buys at our house. It was just something we worked around, like a woman who shops past her credit limit or a workaholic who justifies the hours away from family. If he got busted, we'd deal with it.

Andy was consumed with finding a new Helen, or at least a playmate. He propositioned waitresses and cashiers. He traded in his comfortable Caddy for a red sports car. He continued to attend church, but not for spiritual inspiration. His congregation was well populated by spinsters and widows who lined up with muffins, pies, big hugs, and sexual offers for the newest eligible bachelor. Friends with benefits. Andy accepted their sweets and hugs with increasing anticipation. Jay was mortified.

A lot of the time, I felt like a single mom with three children, Jake, Eli, and Andy. At least they all took naps at the same time most days.

One day about six months after Helen died, I was enjoying a rare moment in a quiet house. Andy hadn't arrived yet; the boys were at pre-school and kindergarten; Jay was on a sales call. The windows were open and the breeze was warm. I was folding clothes at the dining room table when the phone rang. A stranger on the other end identified herself as a nurse from the University of Wisconsin Hospital and asked to speak with Robyn Landon.

Landon? I hadn't used that name in twelve years.

"This is she," I replied, waiting for the fund-raising pitch.

"Your mother is here. She has been in an accident. When we asked her who to contact, this is the only phone number she could recall."

No! No! No! My God, no! was all I could think.

"There was significant trauma to her skull," the nurse continued. "Her cranium has been fractured, and we are still running some tests."

I made arrangements to leave for Wisconsin the same day.

I was prepared for the worst. She'd die or be a vegetable or have amnesia and wouldn't recognize me. Phone calls pinged across the country with family members. We all feared she wouldn't be a genius anymore, and that would be really hard to live with. She was the recognized savant of the family, and she liked being brilliant. I hoped that if she wasn't a brainiac anymore, at least she wouldn't remember that she used to be.

I walked into the hospital room and found her sitting up, fully dressed, with makeup on. "How. Are. You?" I asked slowly, just in case she didn't know English anymore.

"I have a headache, but I'm ready to go home. Want to see my stitches?" she asked mischievously. Hidden behind the hair framing her face, running ear to ear over the top of her head, was a jagged line of blackened dried blood, held together by staples every quarter-inch or so. At the very crown of her head was a shallow, circular hollow where the ball of a 40-foot flagpole had bonked her on the bean, essentially cracking her head in half.

She had been out power walking with another woman in her condo association. After a vigorous hour, they stopped to talk in the driveway of the complex before heading their separate ways. A crane operator was removing the flagpoles lining the entrance of the complex to make room for a wider roadway. As he brought one out of the ground, he lost control of it—instead of coming straight up out of the ground, as it was supposed to, it fell lazily toward the road where my mom was standing, her back to the flagpole. The woman with whom she was in conversation froze, watching as the flagpole came toward them. The ball of the pole crashed into Mom's head, bounced off, and fell to the asphalt. Mom went down immediately but remained in a dazed consciousness. Some one called 9-1-1, and she was whisked to the University of Wisconsin Hospital ER to become a curiosity for all the interns and residents. They cleaned the wound, stapled her skull back together, and called me to retrieve her.

Once we got back to her condo, the neighbors streamed in with questions, casseroles, apologies, and names of ambitious attorneys. While Mom held court with her visitors, I called family members to assure them that Grandma G was still a genius.

While she recuperated, we had some time to talk about the whys of life. What a luxury—time without toddlers' demands, Andy's interruptions, or my husband's depression to consider. Time to spend together, just the two of us. We were both so very grateful for the miracle of her survival, which led to conversations about God and faith, conversations we had skirted in the past. I told her what I had been learning at my church and in my Bible study and what I knew to be true about God. I asked her what she believed about God. She had referred to a Superior Being when I was a kid, more or less an expression of agnosticism. I had always hoped that at some point in her childhood or adolescence, she had acknowledged God in some form. I dared to dream that she had called on the Name of Jesus at some point in her life and might look to him again. I was looking for the loophole that would provide her the key to enter the gates of heaven.

Mom was hesitant to speak at all of things spiritual, for fear her questions and obstacles might undermine my faith. I assured her that even though it had taken me thirty years to tell her that I liked and even wore the color pink, my faith in God through Jesus' death and resurrection was firmly cemented in place.

The long and short of her belief was that, while she was delighted I had "found God" and she saw monumental changes in me that she attributed to my faith in God, she had too many intellectual questions that couldn't be answered and that prevented her from finding a personal faith in a specific deity.

I went so far as to suggest that the bonk on the head, without any apparent long-term effects, was perhaps God's way of getting her attention. "That seems malicious of him," she responded. "I'm not interested in a God who would bash open my head to get my attention." As I saw it, God had saved her life so she would have yet another opportunity to find him. She didn't see the flagpole falling on her as a sign from above that she should surrender her life—even if I did. Stalemate.

Her head healed quickly, the million staples all came out, and her hair filled in around the scar. But the brutal headaches continued throughout her disability leave and afterward as well. She went back to work a full inch shorter, which she fussed about considerably. There was a lump at the base of her neck where the vertebra had been compressed, but she suffered no paralysis and no memory loss.

Back in Michigan, Andy suffered another major heart attack. His doctors advised us that he would need even more help than before. His driving would be limited, his diet had to be monitored—in short, he couldn't live on his own anymore. He had nursing home insurance, but he didn't need a nursing home. He needed assistance. He made too much money with his pension to qualify for government help, but the cost of full-time, in-home care or of an assisted-living facility was beyond his pension. Until his house sold, relieving him of the mortgage payment and returning his equity, we had no other choice. He would have to move in with us.

No No No No No! This can't be happening. It was the line in the sand I had worked so diligently to not let him cross.

But there it was. My choice was to take the chance that he would die alone in his house or bring him home to live in ours. What could I do? He moved in with us.

Our house had a room on the main floor that we used for a TV room, but the previous owners had used it as their bedroom. It had a large closet by farmhouse standards, plus a linen closet, and an attached bathroom—the only bathroom in our house with a shower, but the boys were still taking baths because it was such an excellent time waster, and I had been a bathtub girl for years. We ordered a hospital bed, hooked up Andy's TV, scooped up his clothes and a few personal items, and he called our house home.

He was in heaven.

That's where I wished he was too.

Arrgghhh! It was bad on so many levels! I couldn't fathom how I would be able to tolerate him underfoot all day, every day. My boys were six and three, and I considered them a full-time job. Jay was barely functioning; his grief was still so heavy. He still spent a lot of his time in seclusion.

Since Helen's death, Andy had gained even more weight, tipping the scales at over 350 pounds. His weight inhibited his mobility, and we were all on call to get his coffee, find his remote, or help him put on his socks.

Lack of exercise and too much to eat had affected more than his heart. He tired easily and slept like a wolf, taking lots of naps during the day, leaving him relatively rested at bedtime. He often called for help, company, or a snack in the wee hours of the night. If no one responded, he would sneak upstairs and rub the children's heads till they woke up and cried, which would of course wake me up, at which point Andy would ask me to fulfill whatever request had gone unanswered. "Since you're up anyway," he would say.

His joints swelled, his internal organs labored—even eating was an effort. But at every meal, I watched Andy labor to chew and swallow enough food to feed three adults. Consequently, he was in and out of the hospital and doctors' offices regularly.

But mine was the hand that pushed the grocery cart, and under my watchful eye his health stabilized. He ate mostly nutritious food, even if in oversized portions. I put us all on his special diet to give him a sense of normalcy and inclusion. He took the pills he was supposed to when he was supposed to. He sneaked a treat from time to time, but there wasn't much available to gorge on in my kitchen, so he lost weight and gained energy.

My only respite was a weekly Bible study where I could leave my life for two hours to hear and study God's Word with other women. It was during one of the lessons that I found verses 21–22 in Proverbs 25.

> If your enemy is hungry, give him food to eat;
> if he is thirsty, give him water to drink.
> In doing this, you will heap burning coals on his head,
> and the LORD will reward you.

RIGHT ON! Burning coals for Andy and a reward for me! What's not to like? I kept feeding him and making his coffee and taking him with us everywhere, but I didn't see any burning-coal consequences for him, and I sensed *no reward* for me. If you're taking notes, write this down: If you are a whiner like I was, stay out of the Bible!

After complaining to God about Andy for the millionth time, I found another Scripture passage, Matthew 25:35–40. Jesus is talking to a crowd, and he says, "For I was hungry and you gave me something to eat, I was thirsty and you gave me something to drink, I was a stranger and you invited me in, I needed clothes and you clothed me, I was sick and you looked after me."

When the crowd asks him when they had done all that, Jesus answers, "Truly I tell you, whatever you did for one of the least of these brothers and sisters of mine, you did for me."

Oh no! Feeding and watering for a reward is much different than feeding and watering to serve *Jesus*! The burning coals were falling on *my* head!

Worse yet, I suspected God wasn't planning to take Andy out of my house till I learned this principle! So learn it I did.

I treated Andy as if Jesus Christ himself was walking around with me, taking notes. I imagined Jesus following me with a scroll and quill pen, writing down my every word and action with footnotes about my attitude and motive. That whipped me into shape. I was slower to speak, judge, criticize, or complain. Andy still went everywhere I went. He still got pushy with punks. He still ate prodigious amounts of food with his mouth open. He still sneaked treats to the kids. But I minded less and less. I came to see that Andy was a good man, just desperately lonely and maybe just a bit simple. He needed someone to take care of him in love. Who doesn't?

His vigor was returning, and just when his house sold, he was given a clean bill of health to drive and cavort. He moved out of our guest suite and into an assisted-living facility with a restaurant-quality dining room, not to mention a staff of adorable young aides. Someone else was cleaning his gross bathroom and listening to him complain about whatever was stuck in his craw that day. A beautiful reprieve.

It didn't work out.

We moved him to a different place, and another, and another. It always ended the same way. Andy would get too friendly with the female staff, or drink with the cleaning folks, or get into a fight with someone, and we'd have to move him again.

About the same time, my mom was scheduled to take a trip to Peru. The closer to retirement she got, the more time she took off, much of it to travel. The trip she had taken to China the year before had been so exciting that she was done with ordinary destinations. She would never see America through the windshield of an RV or retire to a trailer park in Florida or Arizona—even if they *were* called resorts. It was penthouse condos for her, within walking distance to the theater, bistros, and coffee shops. She bought most of her clothes from catalogues, so she didn't need to be close to malls or supermarkets. She drove a racy little BMW convertible that was easy to park in underground garages or on the streets of any metropolis.

I had no desire to travel to Peru, but my life's intrigue consisted of taking care of Andy, taking care of youngsters, and coaxing my depressed husband out of his office for dinner, so I listened raptly as she described her itinerary, the new wrinkle-resistant travel clothes she'd found, and the sights she was eager to visit.

As a precaution, she scheduled a well-woman checkup with her doctor. Routine blood tests revealed abnormalities. Blood cells and counts and shapes were askew on the little slides under the microscope at the office laboratory.

Cancer.

She was sent home to put anything in order that wasn't already and then report to the Oncology Ward of the University of Wisconsin Hospital.

"Right. I'll do that as soon as I get home from Peru."

"Dr. Landon, perhaps you don't understand the seriousness of your condition. You need to be in the hospital within twenty-four hours."

She called me from the doctor's office, using her "this is serious" voice but trying not to sound worried. We both said things to make the other feel better, like, "Well, they caught it early," and "Maybe it's a misdiagnosis," and "The U.W. hospital is one of the best in the country—and you can visit the nice people who stapled your head back in place."

The diagnosis was acute leukemia—cancer of the blood. The protocol to combat it is to kill everything good *and* bad in your blood, and hope that all the nasty leukemias have been annihilated when the cells grow back. To protect her compromised immune system during the five week long rounds of chemo, she was quarantined in the hospital's blood cancer ward.

I would go to Madison to stay with her during her hospitalized treatments, alternating weeks with my brother. Except for her being so sick, it was wonderful. I believed medical science could cure anything if caught in the early stages, and I got to spend all that time alone with her in the middle of my busy life. I left behind my husband who had withdrawn into his work and marijuana to grieve, my preschooler and kindergartner, all the papers from their schools, the phone calls from Andy about women, car accidents, and doctor appointments. I spent my days at the hospital with my mom eating chocolate, watching movies, and talking about anything and everything. Mom paid for my flights and gave me "walking around money."

The medical staff was top-notch, but I was her personal caregiver. I cherished the time I had her to myself, petting her, singing to her, battling body-wracking chills with hot compresses. We talked of things past and present and future. Laughter occasionally burbled out, even there. I prayed aloud and she listened. I watched and waited for her to get better or die.

The treatment of her cancer was aggressive. Her body lay wasted, her nearly translucent skin poked full of small holes from a million needles. Her eyes were sunken in their sockets, a condition exaggerated by the absence of makeup and by sleep deprivation. Her smile faded, and her excitement in everything waned. It was a full-time job to survive each day, enduring the treatments and the side effects, conquering the fear of doing it all over again the next day if she lived through the night.

She was a captive audience, and I talked to her about the simplicity of following Jesus. I remember thinking, *Lord, just put someone in her path she respects enough to listen to. And, Lord, lead her to a book or a study that piques her interest in spiritual things. Finally, Lord, show yourself to her. Show her your love and mercy; let her know your peace. Heal her and let her know you are God!* Between movies and chemo treatments, pictorial presentations of the kids, and lamenting Andy's latest antics, I told her about my life following Jesus. I told her I had more balance and more joy, even though I was juggling some really difficult people and circumstances. I told her about the women in my life who were picking up the slack for me while I was gone, dropping off meals and collecting kids. I told her about what I was learning in my Bible study class. I told her I had fewer triggers to frustrations. I acted less and less like a spoiled toddler when frustrated, having gained patience and kindness as a result of the gift of love Jesus poured out on me—and that had been exhibited to me by the lovely women in my class. I hoped that she would be moved to receive Jesus as I had. She listened without effect, sticking to her vapor-spirit-recycling theory: we all belong to a huge mass of energy and we're sort of recycled when we die.

Mom went through months and months of treatment before her counts were acceptable and she could resume her life.

Remission was my new favorite word.

Without me as his steady companion, Andy was out and about, feasting on fried food and doughnuts, and the weight piled back on. He probably shouldn't have been driving, but he passed the state tests and the assisted-living facilities provided parking spaces for his red babe-magnet.

He slid in and out of depression. He "forgot" to take the medicine that kept him alive, and his health dissolved again. He had lost or given up everything that made him feel important. He wasn't a cop or a worker, he wasn't somebody's husband or somebody's Romeo—he wasn't even king of his own castle. Being sick gave him purpose; it legitimized his life.

For months and months, Jay and I had one or both parents in the hospital, in separate states.

As Andy got evicted from place after place, we kept trying to find him spots to accommodate the level of care he needed, with brief stays at our house. He didn't want to live in any of the places we found. He would deliberately sink below whatever level of care he was given, and he pushed the limits of the staff's tolerance. He was determined to get Jay to rescue him and bring him back home to live with us permanently.

The seventh move was the charm. He finally landed at a place with some spry, silver-haired women residents and a director who must have been descended from angels, because even when Andy was naughty, she would gently correct him and they would make a truce. Stonebridge was an assisted-living facility, but the amount of assistance depended on what their clients needed from day to day.

By this time, Andy had lost his driving privileges, but they let him keep the sporty red ride in the parking lot for show. The grounds were full of ponds and wildlife. Andy could fish or sit in pseudo wilderness. He still complained about the food, which is to say that it wasn't loaded with fat and sugar. His weight kept melting off and his medications were correspondingly reduced. There was an upscale grocery store and deli about two blocks from Stonebridge, and Andy took to walking there for his sneaky treats—for which the lovely people at Stonebridge never scolded him. He was using a walker when he moved in, but after a bit, it sat dusty in the corner except to use as a grocery cart for his bounty from the store.

All that walking was good for him. He was looking better and feeling better than I had ever seen him. He dropped a ton of weight chasing the walker to the store. He was even more sensitive and charming, generous and thoughtful. Now that someone else was feeding him and cleaning him and his domicile, even doing his laundry, I really enjoyed his company. We "ran the roads" together, as he put it—going to restaurants, swimming at the pool, volunteering at the kids' school, exchanging playful banter with the cashiers at the grocery store.

For six whole weeks, the world was a wondrous place. It had been a long time since all was well with our world, but it seemed to be back on its axis. Jay was still smoking pot regularly, but his despair was lifting. He volunteered us to lead the fifth-grade Sunday school class at church. He was climbing out of the blackness that had oppressed him since his mom died eighteen months earlier. He no longer seemed disengaged and angry. He laughed, he played with the boys; there was new confidence in his sales calls.

Then Andy had a massive stroke. He was partially paralyzed. He couldn't talk. He was too severely handicapped to return to Stonebridge or even go to a nursing home. He was moved to a rehab hospital—which was crowded and understaffed and operated without the amenities common to traditional hospitals. The old beds had cranks instead of buttons to raise and lower them; there were no phones in the rooms or televisions suspended from the ceiling. Even if the call buttons worked, no one came. The rooms on his floor were small and colorless, permeated with the smell of despair. It was a vacuum of hopelessness, a warehouse to store people until they gave up and died.

Jay hated the place and avoided going to visit, but I went there every day. Accustomed as I was to spending whole days and nights in the hospital with Mom during her bout with leukemia, sitting with Andy for a couple of hours while the kids were in school was no hardship. I tried to get him to eat, but he wouldn't take a bite. I washed the crusties out of his eyes and from around his mouth with warm cloths. I sponged his head and neck and hands with warm water and put Corn Huskers Lotion on him. (Andy had always liked the feel and smell of it, though I called it elephant snot.) I told him charming stories about the children, but his smile was gone. His eyes hardly flickered. I stroked his big old bald head and patted the fat fingers of his hands while I quietly sang old hymns to him. I whispered in his ear that he was loved.

Then Andy gave up. He decided there wasn't anything to live for, and he willed himself to death.

When Andy died, we were sad, but I'm not going to lie—I was relieved too. He was in heaven with his Savior, he was reunited with Helen, and even though I know there is no marriage in heaven, I like to think she was appointed to be his heavenly tour guide.

And me? I experienced God's pleasure with me! I felt like I had run the good race, passed the test, claimed the prize. Victory in Jesus, baby! Back to normal life! Fancy underwear night is back!

Chapter 9

FUNERALS AND BIRTHDAYS

Andy's death meant I spent my fortieth birthday at the funeral parlor. Almost no one wished me happy birthday, which was really disappointing since I look forward to my birthday *season* with childlike eagerness. I need more than one day to celebrate, so I had created my own season full of lunches and rendezvous with friends and family. That year, though, it seemed rude and selfish to make birthday arrangements in light of Andy's death. So my big 4-0 birthday season was forfeited.

Jay's brothers and sister, along with their families, came for Andy's funeral, but not one of Andy's siblings nor anyone else from his nuclear family made the trip to Grand Rapids. My mom who—Glory Hallelujah!—was healthy enough to travel came sporting a blonde wig. Craig flew over in his little plane. Members of my church family filled the service with flowers and well wishes.

With Andy gone, it was just the four of us again. Jay, Jake, Eli, and me. It was delightfully quiet and pleasantly mundane. *Peaceful* was the default condition.

Saturdays were easy at our house. The boys watched cartoons and Jay often watched with them. If they tired of sitting on his warm lap or got into a scrap, the crate of Matchbox cars and long orange plastic sections of track would come out and Jay would build a looping, swooping course for the boys to see whose car would go the farthest and the fastest. Other mornings, Duplos and Legos spilled out of storage tubs the size of water heaters, and Jay would either build some colorful architecture with them or search for the one missing piece that was crucial to complete their art prize. Some Saturdays the green army men fought against the tan army men, or all the army men would stage an offensive against the Teenage Mutant Ninja Turtles.

Three weeks after Andy's funeral, Mom flew into town for a real visit with us. Her long stays in the hospital to combat leukemia had left her with a phobia about germs. She became accustomed to living quarantined in white, sterile environs. No plants or even fresh fruit were allowed anywhere near her during the cancer treatments. Travel to Andy's funeral had been by car, with few opportunities for contamination. She kept a distance from people, washed her hands frequently, and tried not to let her fear of germs consume her.

This trip, she braved traffic and airports to show her shockingly short hair to my little boys, who were astonished that those despicable leukemias had stolen the yellow right out of Grandma G's hair! Her hair didn't look happy anymore. It was fascinating to hear her tell about the evil magic that had caused the yellow waves to give way to the boring salt-and-pepper stubble she sported. The boys wanted to know if the yellow would ever come back. "Maybe," she said with a wink at me.

Her plane arrived in Grand Rapids on a Friday night, and the whole family went to the airport to collect her. Jake and Eli normally went to bed at 7:30 p.m., but we allowed them to stay up a bit later than usual to go to the airport. This was pre-9/11, and we were able to go all the way to her arrival gate, our usual practice when Mom flew in for a visit. On each trip, we would watch the small commercial jet taxi to the gate. Standing at the exit door of the plane on the tarmac as she disembarked, she'd search the windows of the terminal for us and wave like a crazy woman. Then she would walk across the tarmac to the terminal and climb the one flight of stairs to our gate.

At the top of the stairs, she would drop everything she carried and scoop up whoever could get to her first. Once we were all properly schmooshed and sniffed and declared bigger or more beautiful than last time, we went back to the airport terminal window so she could point out to the children "her" airplane and tell them where she'd sat, how turbulent was the wind, the names of the crew—and then she would declare that she was *so* glad to be right here! Once at the house, Mom would settle into the guest room and dispense to the boys trinkets gathered during her travels.

With Granny Helen (Jay's mom) dead for over a year and Grandpa Andy-with-the-Big-Belly (Jay's dad) in the grave only three weeks, grandparents were suddenly a rare commodity, and Mom's visit seemed like a promise of a return to normalcy. To days that weren't filled with doctor appointments and emergency rooms, phone calls of bad news, trauma. Grandma G considered Jake and Eli, at seven and four, the perfect age to play with. Both were healthy, smiled easily, and laughed often—but more importantly they were potty trained, speaking in full sentences, and completely gullible.

On past winter visits, Mom had gotten up super early, filled squirt bottles with water dyed with food colors, and sketched gnome twins in the snow (because as everyone knows, gnomes always come in sets), as if gnomes had been there and left shadowy impressions of themselves. This discovery of gnome sign would lead to a hunt for the gnomes themselves. While the mystical creatures would elude the boys, they would find chocolate bars and marshmallows, making it a banner quest.

Other times, she led them on adventure hikes around the neighborhood, regaling them with stories about the inhabitants of various homes who were not human at all, but who had been hatched from fuzzballs and lived among the humans in fear of being found out. They were gentle aliens with green blood who lived for hundreds of years. Their plan was to establish residency on our planet by infiltrating and cross-pollinating with earthlings. In exchange for asylum, the fuzzball people would share the great secrets of long life and peaceful cohabitation. Unfortunately, the warmongering Republicans rejected the fuzzball people's request, so they lived in constant fear of being exposed. Grandma G persuaded the children to keep the fuzzballs' secret at least until the Republicans were out of office.

Bedtimes weren't complete without a Gobbernopper story, ongoing sagas of the Gobbernopper family, which, of course, had a mama Gobbernopper who looked and acted just like me, and a daddy Gobbernopper, who was a caricature of Jay, a giant of a man who protected his wife and children against enemies with an arsenal of weaponry and vanquished all monstrous marauders. There were two Gobbernopper children, Jacob Gobbernopper and Eli Gobbernopper, who were always the avenging and conquering heroes. They had superpowers, including but not limited to mind reading and the ability to fly, in addition to the super-strength they inherited from Father Gobbernopper and the brilliant intelligence they inherited from Grandma Gobbernopper. Mom would weave herself into the narratives as a wizard or sage to aid the heroes against pernicious attacks from evil forces.

She painted snakes and dragons and butterfly tattoos on the boys' torsos. She clomped around in my heavy winter boots and donned a bright sash to sheath her sword, an oversized sharpening steel, leftover from my grandpa's butcher shop.

Grandma G was the bomb.

It was hard to believe this woman, who was messy and carefree, who made sand pies in my kitchen and gave children red Kool-Aid in open-top cups, was the same woman who had raised me, or even the same woman who now lived alone in a pristine condominium in Madison, Wisconsin.

Obviously, grandparenting comes with privileges and remission bestows fresh starts.

Mom's condo in Madison was fit for a magazine layout: immaculate white walls and carpet accentuated by twin miniaturized black sofas that formed an S in front of a floor-to-ceiling, blanched-stone fireplace. Despite all the light that filtered into the room through skylights and huge double sets of French doors, the high-gloss, black baby grand never had so much as a fleck of dust. Stone gargoyles sat comfortably on the hearth, Easter Island–like stone carved heads kept watch over the open, sterile kitchen, two foreboding iron dragons the size of toddlers perched on oddly shaped display stands like sentries, and oversized gray-and-steel-blue wall pieces of metal hung on the white walls.

At my house, Mom was completely at home with me and my children, my lumpy, mismatched couches, and my eclectic collection of lamps and tables. There were several antique bookcases and a library table and dining room hutch that Helen had contributed. The oak pedestal table that had anchored every holiday at my grandma's house since 1932 now graced my dining room. My Grandma and Grandpa Clark bought it out of the Sears catalogue as newlyweds. I claimed the table and chairs rather than the monetary inheritance the other cousins got. Jay was not thrilled. He had never warmed to my Grandma Clark and didn't want any of her bad mojo dragged into our house. He permitted the table on a trial basis, moving the table we already owned into the living room until a winner could be decided. It took almost a year before he parted with the one in the living room. Visitors questioned our decorating savvy, but everyone always had a place to sit for meals.

On the Friday night of Mom's arrival, Jay sat in the TV room and watched television while Mom and I talked in the living room until we were exhausted and went to bed. I kissed Jay good night and went up to the bedroom before him, as I did many nights. I needed more sleep than he did, and night was his alone time. Since Jay worked from an office at home, he had to frequently and on short notice take off his Salesman hat and put on his Family Man hat. He flowed from one role to the other easily, but everyone needs a break, and late night was his time to relax, smoke in the house, and snack in front of the TV.

Jacob was up once that night with a headache. I tiptoed downstairs to get him some children's pain reliever and saw that Jay was asleep on the couch. I turned off the television, hoping he would wake up so I could steer him toward bed. He didn't. I debated waking him, but I knew if I woke him at 4:00 a.m., there was a good possibility he wouldn't be able to get back to sleep and would be grumpy. I decided to leave him there, took the medicine to Jake, and went back to bed by myself.

Saturday unfolded as the weatherman had predicted, no small feat in Michigan where weather changes are constant. The sun was out, the sky was clear, and it was unseasonably warm, an Indian Summer day—an unexpected delight when children can go outside to blow bubbles, jump in leaves, or chase squirrels. It was exactly the kind of day mothers of young children love: the last hurrah before a long winter of indoor activities and layers of clothing every day. It was perfect for one last trike and hike with Grandma G before all the outdoor toys with wheels would be stored in the loft of the garage for the winter.

The boys were up early and scarfed their breakfast so they could start their adventures with Grandma G. "How's your head this morning?" I asked Jake.

"Oh—I forgot all about it. It must be gone, Mom. I'm ready to play with Grandma G!"

Jay, who often ate what we all called second supper in front of late-night television, rarely ate breakfast. True to form, the leftovers from last night's dinner had disappeared from the refrigerator, and a plate with bare chicken bones and traces of gravy sat on the coffee table.

While I washed the breakfast dishes and chatted with Mom, both boys watched TV in the room where Jay slept. Good, finally some decent rest for him. The past year had been so hard on him—taking care of Andy, still missing his mom so badly, then planning Andy's funeral and hosting the out-of-town guests; me spending weeks at a time away from home with Mom during her chemo treatments. Even with a sitter during the day, there had still been a lot for Jay to do while I'd been gone: juggling kids, the house, his dad's emergencies, and a full-time job had exhausted him.

But today Mom's plans to take the kids outside would mean Jay would have some daytime peace and quiet to drink his coffee, smoke cigarettes, and even read the newspaper. I considered leaving a note, then decided he would want to know he had the house to himself. I went into the TV room to tell him we were leaving.

I stood in front of Jay, who was sleeping on the couch. He looked rested. The television was on behind me, an innocuous sing-song show; Eli lay on the carpet near me, mesmerized by the magic of television. I could hear Jake and my mom chattering in the kitchen, excitedly developing a villainous character to vanquish. Jake's arsenal of wooden swords and rubber-band guns would play some part in the impending destruction of despots in my front yard. "Eli, go see what Grandma G and Jake are planning, will you, please?" I said. "I think we're going for a walk outside. You can ride your bike."

He was off and away to the kitchen.

Jay had taken a shower late the night before; his hair was clean and shiny, his clothes were clean, he looked like a little boy. *God,* I thought as I looked at my peacefully sleeping husband, *I sure do love this man.* Leaning closer, I caught the smell of soap and Old Spice. I whispered his name. No response. *Wow, he's pale; he needs some sun.* Like a character on a TV drama, I put two fingers against his neck to check for a pulse. Since I can't even find my *own* heartbeat unless I've just finished an aerobic workout, I wasn't alarmed when I didn't find his. A resting pulse would be tricky to locate. I put my whole hand on his forehead to check for a fever.

He was cold.

I screamed Jay's name and pounded his chest with both fists. There was no give; his body was hard. I yelled for both kids and shouted for my mom to call 9-1-1. No sooner had the kids rushed in than I decided they shouldn't see him, so I sent them to their rooms—then I decided I didn't want them to be alone and didn't want them out of my sight, so I yelled for them to come back. By this time Mom had the 9-1-1 dispatcher on the phone. She handed it to me and ushered the kids into another part of the house.

The dispatcher calmly instructed me to put Jay on the floor so I could administer CPR until the police arrived. I tried to move him, but he outweighed me by a hundred pounds. "I can't move him! He weighs too much!" I cried frantically, but she insisted that I try to at least move him into a proper position for CPR. As I tried to pull him onto his back, his shirt twisted open, exposing his torso. There was what looked like a huge bruise on his left side. Gravity had drawn the uncirculating blood down into the side of his body that had been lying against the couch.

Fire trucks arrived; firemen in full firefighting regalia poured into our home. An ambulance appeared, and men in starched white shirts dotted with embroidered patches examined Jay.

"He's cold and his body is hard and there's a pool of blood in his belly!" I cried. I didn't need to ask if there was anything they could do.

An EMT examined Jay's body thoroughly and gently told me what I already knew. Jay was dead.

The EMT straightened Jay's clothes and positioned his body on the couch in a not-quite-sitting position. "The coroner will be here soon to pronounce time of death," the EMT said. "If you want to spend any time with him or say good-bye, you could do that now."

I wanted to crawl into Jay's lap and stay there. Let them bury both of us. How could I live without him? He looked just as strong and powerful dead as he had the night before. He looked peaceful. There was no death in the air.

His hands were my favorite part of him. I held them and sobbed, because for the first time in the twenty-one years I'd known him, they were cold.

There was a lot of shuffling around. Heroic men, trapped in the moment, helpless to change the circumstances and helpless in the face of a family's grief, hovered in the adjacent rooms. One firefighter brought in a stuffed teddy bear for each of the boys, such a kind gesture, but even as the strapping young man in uniform handed the toys to them, he seemed to understand the gifts' inadequacy. My boys had never wanted dolls, ever, and today of all days, what they wanted was for their dad to be alive. They said an awkward thank you and disappeared.

Forced to stay put until a commander somewhere released them, the firefighters, police, and ambulance team idled about. After some time, hours maybe, the men in uniform began exiting in the order they had come, the firefighters saying an uncomfortable good-bye first, then all but one policeman. The EMTs remained. The coroner came. He wore black and his jacket had CORONER in white letters on the back.

I had to leave the room while he examined Jay. I sat on the floor outside the TV room, hugging my legs, my head on my knees, rocking myself like a terrified child. We had been together for so long, I thought we were fused. When he died, why hadn't I too? What would I do without him? How would I get along? A teeny tiny quiet thought ran through my mind: *You will be fine—trust me. Trust me. You'll be okay. I know you don't like this, but you are ready for it. Jay is with me, and I am always with you.* A calm started to settle on me like a warm fuzzy blanket. I was still shaking, but I kept hearing that reassurance of the Holy Spirit of God: *You'll be okay. Just trust me. You don't lose your joy even when you lose important people. I am your joy.*

The coroner came back from his examination. I didn't mention Jay's use of pot. I did ask about not waking him at 4:00 a.m. "Did I ruin his chances by not trying to wake him earlier and calling for help then?"

"Jay has been dead since at least 2:00 a.m.," he said. "And even if you had walked into the room with an EMT at the instant of his heart attack, nothing would have saved his life. He was dead in less than two seconds. A heart attack of such proportion is fatal every time."

How he knew all that, I don't know, but he said exactly what I needed to hear: *There was nothing you could have done.*

The autopsy revealed that Jay had almost 90 percent blockage in all the arteries in his heart, and that he had suffered at least one other heart attack that had gone untreated. Jay had been predisposed to pass early, given his family history—that is, his mom dying of a heart attack and his dad's multiple heart attacks and stroke. He smoked two packs of cigarettes a day and had high blood pressure—the heart attack was inevitable.

Jay was gone and I was alone. I'd thought when we buried Andy that I was done with the trial. I had learned to trust God and listen for him. Turns out, I was only being prepped for the future.

Chapter 10

LOUSY
TRADE-OFFS

Death is something that's supposed to happen to old dogs and very old people. And preferably in the distant future. Death visited me unexpectedly. I never saw it coming.

Jay and I had been married barely fourteen years when he died. In the span of a night's sleep, everything in my world shifted. In the time it takes for the moon to cross the sky, my life, and the lives of my two children, changed forever.

I wouldn't wish the pain I felt on my worst enemy. It felt like a cannonball-sized hole had been blown right through the center of me, and I couldn't understand why I was still upright and taking oxygen. I wanted everything to just stop for a moment so I could get my footing. I was sure I could feel the earth spinning under me.

Fortunately, our church family rallied to our aid. Our pastor, as well as friends from my Bible study, arrived at the house before the body was removed. Women came in droves to sit with me, to pray with me, to love on me. A few became pillars, women who stayed with me for the long haul. I didn't have the energy for high-maintenance relationships; my pillars were women who had been a part of my life before Jay died and stuck with me through the entire grieving process. These women answered their phones in the middle of the night. They helped me figure out how to get my oil changed, bought me a season of lawn service, and celebrated high occasions like wedding anniversaries and birthdays with me. Other women decorated my life for a season, like Christmas lights in December or a table centerpiece for a party. They swooped in with chicken salad sandwiches, circus tickets, or children's books and then were gone. All these women mitigated the suffering.

I hated doing the boy jobs: the driving, carrying, toting, and hauling. I hated shoveling the sidewalk and raking the yard. I hated cars that wouldn't start and I hated reading maps. I hated sitting alone in church. I hated calling every utility company, credit card company, and magazine subscription to take Jay's name off the account. I hated figuring out how to buy insurance for cars and homes and people. I hated parenting alone.

I knew Jay would have stayed if he could have. He would have kept our agreement to take the boys to the garage at the proper age to teach them about all things mechanical. He would have taught them how to drive and how to treat women. He would have shown them how to tie a Windsor knot and spit-polish shoes and fix a leaky faucet and a thousand other things that an Andraszczyk man needs to know. He didn't get the chance. It's odd to think that he doesn't mind about missing those things. Because I minded. I minded a lot. I missed his voice of reason in my emotional meltdowns, his reinforcement with stubborn children, his financial acumen, his radar for bull, his wizardry for fixing things. I missed his skilled and tender hand on me, on my life, on our boys.

There is a way to grieve, and while there are some universal components, it's as individual as your mama's chili. I had good days. Other days, I was so sad groans substituted for words. There were fleeting moments of fear about being alone, parenting alone, what to do for money when the life insurance was gone. Jay had been a terrific husband. The grinding singleness, the oneness of being one instead of being one with a husband, was an unwelcome reality.

In the uncharted territory of grieving, well-intentioned people said hurtful things. Women confronted me in the ladies' room at church. They stopped me in the grocery store and at the hair salon.

"How can you carry on?"

"You seem so happy. Did you *really* love him?"

"Do you think he'd approve of the way you're changing his house?"

"Are you losing weight to attract a new husband?"

"Was there some sin that needed to be acknowledged?"

I believe that most of the people who maimed me didn't know what to say. In their ignorance and inexperience, they simply said the wrong thing. Hollywood filled the protocol gap. It felt like there was an expectation from some congregants at my church that I wear black, and maybe a veil, for at least a year, during which time I should languish in despair.

I decided to be gracious to the confused. Forgiving of the snipers. I comforted those perplexed by my situation. I can only explain my responses by saying that God overwhelmed me with his grace, infiltrating me, speaking through me. I was able to smile, encourage, even console others at the height of my grief.

I found solace in God's perfect timing. Jake and Eli, at seven and four, were walking, talking, sleeping through the night, and potty trained. Young enough to be resilient and old enough to have their father's fine character qualities etched on them for life.

Jay died three weeks after his father. It would not have been so far-fetched to believe that Andy would have wanted to step into Jay's empty shoes. How awkward would that conversation have been? Beyond not having to fend off Andy's advances, I didn't have to make decisions about Andy's funeral, burial site, or estate disbursements, or move his few remaining belongs by myself.

Jay died at home. I had hours and hours to say good-bye.

He traveled for work, so I had already been coached (in case of an accident) on whom to call, what to sell, and what to keep. I was absolutely *not* to get rid of any tools or the compressor or the hydraulic jacks, as Jay was certain the boys would use them someday. I was to stay in the house for at least a year (to keep my mom from running my life). I was to bury him in the cemetery across the street and not spend much on a casket. Because we had just buried Andy and Helen, I didn't even need to look up the number for the funeral parlor; the director and I were on a first-name, speed-dial basis.

As I slogged through my new normal, I heard God's constant assurances. It was just barely enough. But it *was* enough.

⸎

I discovered the gift of the lousy trade-off. My bed was easy to make, but I was sleeping solo.

I never had to make stinky Polish kluskis or Salisbury steak again. Watermelon and Ritz crackers with cheese spread could be a meal if I wanted. I could go out for dinner whenever I pleased. But there was an empty chair at the table.

My mouth was dry all the time—chewing and swallowing was an effort. I had no appetite; weight fell off me. The thirty-odd pounds I had put on to make a home for babies in my womb and cuddle toddlers after naps melted off. I was model-skinny again but single and sad.

Jake and Eli functioned pretty well. Friends invited them on lots of play dates. They ate at McDonald's and spent hours in the playland there. They went to the circus to see the clowns and to the orchard for doughnuts and cider. People bought them gifts and fed them candy. They had plenty of attention, but they didn't have a dad.

I used a big chunk of the life insurance money to fix everything about the house I didn't like or had been waiting for Jay to fix to make the house safer or more beautiful. I replaced appliances that didn't work well because Jay wasn't there to keep them running. The first time I put a load of wet clothes in the new dryer, I automatically reached for the stick to prop the old door closed. I actually sang out *Hallelujah!* to celebrate the new door staying shut on its own. I had long-awaited central air conditioning installed because I didn't feel safe leaving the windows open without Jay there to fend off intruders. Plumbers replaced leaky faucets and unclogged water lines. A shiny new bathroom with good water pressure took the place of the moldy, pink-tiled eyesore. Electricians installed lights in closets and outlets in bedrooms. The filthy, rutted gravel driveway disappeared under a smooth river of black asphalt. A big red truck with a scoop made sure it was never covered by snow. A green truck with a big trailer came to mow. Painters and carpenters and insulation specialists appeared, transformed my house, and departed.

I didn't have to wait for anything to *cure* (which is man-speak for *I don't want to do that right now*); I didn't have to save enough money or wait for Jay to have enough time or energy to work on the house—but my little boys didn't have a daddy.

Somewhere during the remodeling process, a worker on break was admiring our family pictures in the den. He stared at a picture of Jay and me taken before children arrived, so to be fair, it was eight or nine years old. "Who's that with your husband?" he asked.

"Oh, that's me," I replied, remembering the day it had been taken.

His head whipped around and he looked at me in disbelief. "You are *kidding*! Doesn't look like you at all."

"Really?" I asked.

"No," he said. "You look really good in that picture."

Completely undone, I went to a mirror. My waist-length hair was pinned up in a tight, figure-eight bun. My skin was blotchy and pale. Without makeup to accentuate them, my pretty green eyes disappeared. My pants were faded and sagged at the knees. My shirt was old and soft from laundering.

I looked like the *mother* of the woman in the picture.

Jay always preferred me with a natural look and long hair, but I had let myself become dowdy. I called my beautician, and when I showed up for my appointment, I said, "Help me feel pretty again!" After a makeover and shampoo, a foot of hair fell to the floor. I bought a closet full of pretty new clothes. I looked great, but there was no husband to appreciate the changes.

Hundreds of people came to Jay's funeral. Pastor Ed Dobson did a wonderful job telling the audience about Jay and about Jesus. We even had some fun at his funeral. Pastor Ed said, "Despite the hundreds of funerals I have officiated or even heard about from other ministers, I have never seen a Green Bay Packers flag draping a casket."

It was important to me that the service be as much about salvation through Jesus' death and resurrection as it was about Jay. I knew there would be people in the audience who would never grace the seats of a church except for command performances like weddings and funerals. To miss the opportunity to tell them about their Savior would have been profusely wasteful.

Instead of telling us what he didn't know about God, Pastor Ed told us what he did. He looked at me and the kids. "I just don't have a good answer today for why this bad thing happened. Jay is not dead; this is just the body he used to walk around in. Jay isn't here anymore. Jay is in the presence of the Lord, not because he was a great fan, friend, or husband or employee. Jay is in heaven because he accepted Jesus as his personal Savior." Several people made a public declaration to receive Jesus as Savior that day and many more told me the service profoundly affected them spiritually. I think many prodigals ran home that day to the open arms of their heavenly Father.

The funeral reception was the best three hours I'd had in a week—or that I would have for a long time. I was surrounded by people who cared about me. I nibbled cake. I heard wonderful stories about my dead husband. I wanted time to stand still.

After the reception, we buried Jay in the cemetery kitty-corner across the street from our house. Jay had wanted his marker to function like the *home free* spot in a child's game of hide-and-seek, a place for his wife and kids and friends to sit or visit, to talk or cry privately.

Craig, Jay's pilot friend and Lambeau Field sod-collecting accomplice, took pictures the entire day. Leave it to him to take snapshots as if he were at a party! The clod. I thought he was so clueless, so inappropriate. I wasn't the only one who thought so—he got the fisheye from many.

After the burial, family and guests drifted back to their own lives or on to the next crisis in the church. The cards stopped filling the mailbox and the phone rang less.

My heart slowly mended. I was lonely without Jay; it stinks being left behind. There were times when the longing for even fifteen minutes of my old life back was so strong that it was physically painful. Eventually, those cravings and desires came farther apart and lost their intensity. Most of our days were pretty good. The children and I remembered Jay as we made new memories without him.

We decided—that is to say, I decided—that we would not have bad days unless someone died. You could have a *piece* of a bad day, but no one was allowed to be grumpy or crabby or sad for the entire day. We used thankfulness to combat the inclination to wallow in sadness. Every night at prayer time we told each other at least one thing that had gone well; we shared what we were thankful for. When the love of your life has been snatched, trust me, it's tempting to use that as an excuse to put on an entitlement crown and sit in a pity pool, throw fits, or demand special treatment. This decision to deliberately choose thankfulness and reap the by-products of peace and joy delighted some and confounded many.

ⁿ◦◦◦

I wanted the boys to remember Jay, but I wanted them to remember him as accurately as possible. I wanted to honor the dead without building him a shrine. I didn't want to make him so perfect that the world or life in general wasn't worth investing in if he wasn't here. I didn't want their lives to stop because Jay's had—like that pilot Craig's had when his dad died. I didn't want them to idolize him. My decision to leave pictures of Jay up and talk openly about him pleased his family, who in fact did very much want me to build an altar to Jay and worship at it.

Four or five months after Jay died, I hit a low spot. The prospect of scores of years ahead of me alone, slogging through lousy trade-offs, was too hard. I allowed myself the luxury of being pitiful. I was not thankful. I did not see blessings. I was being a brat.

A verse a lot of people quote to you when you are in a tough spot is Romans 8:28: "And we know that in all things God works for the good of those who love him, who have been called according to his purpose." So I demanded of God, "I love you, so where's the good for me?"

He answered, "Your bed is easy to make."

What? Really, that's it?

Nothing further was forthcoming from him. I thought about it. It was true. My bed *was* easy to make. When I go to bed, I fold back a corner of the bedding, slip in, replace the covers over me and go to sleep. When I wake up, I unfold the covers, slip out, and the bedding goes right back in place. Jay, on the other hand, tossed and rolled and dreamed of pugilist bouts or thwarting villains, kicking loose the covers from foot of bed to headboard. It was a small thing, but it started me thinking about all the blessings I did have.

One morning, in a big hurry to get on with my day, I scurried both little boys out to the garage and buckled them into their car seats. I backed out of the garage, but when I hit the little button that is supposed to close the garage door, nothing happened. Frustrated, I tried again, but the door stubbornly guffawed. *Grrr.* I couldn't leave the door open because all Jay's precious tools were in there. There was no choice—I would have to get out of the car and close the door manually with the red hang-y-down cord I had seen Jay use during a power outage.

I leapt out of the car to close the garage door and wasn't two steps away from the car before I heard the boys screaming behind me. "MMMMMOOOOOOOMMMMM!"

I turned to see my car, with the children fastened in the backseat, rolling down our long, steep driveway toward the road. I had obviously not put the car in park but in reverse. I pointed my finger at the car and said, "Jesus, Jesus, Jesus, do you see that car? That car has my kids in it. You've got to stop that car! Stop that car right now!"

And he did. The car with the boys in it veered just enough to run off the driveway and smack-dab into the front end of Jay's beautifully restored prized car. I ran to throw open the backseat door of my car. Visibly shaken, the boys were nonetheless safe and sound in their car seats. "Are you okay?" I asked, and then, always thinking on my feet to deflect blame and hopefully avoid years of therapy, I said, "Was that fun?"

They said, "*Don't do that again!*"

I assured them I would not. With the children's safety accounted for, I stepped away from the vehicles to assess the damage. The back of my car was caved in and the front of the trophy car Jay had worked so hard to restore was crunched in. Just for a split-second, I thought, *How am I going to explain this to Jay?* I looked up at the house. Our crashed cars were just outside his home office window. A smile crept across my face. I can honestly say that for the first time I thought, *I am so glad my husband is dead!* There just isn't a good way to tell your husband you've wrecked both the cars and nearly killed his children all in one fell swoop!

Months after the funeral, a package arrived postmarked Milwaukee, Wisconsin. That flaky pilot! What now? Inside the package were dozens of pictures of Jay's funeral. As I looked at those prints, I decided that everyone should hire a photographer to document their funerals. The pictures were full of people I'd forgotten had attended. They captured the pain and the joy, the reverence and the revelry of our communal grief. I arranged the pictures on corkboard above Jay's desk at home. It became my treasure board. I would sit at his desk in the home office, holding his favorite Packers hat up to my face, breathing in the scent of him, and look at those sweet pictures.

Chapter 11

UNDER THE MICROSCOPE

I was so relieved my mom was visiting us the weekend Jay died. Not just because it was such a big help or comfort to have her there, but because she finally experienced what I'd been trying to explain about God for years. Until that weekend, she'd been too smart, too well educated, and too self-sufficient to need God.

After Jesus caught up with me, Mom would visit my church from time to time. She would sing the hymns, mostly by heart (which surprised me), acknowledge the talent of the choir and orchestra, attentively follow the sermon, and smile at her pew mates. And about the time I was starting to think she had been really touched or impacted by the service, she would say, "What a professional show that was. And the child care seems so well organized."

When Jay died, my faith became living proof of a living God. The Holy Spirit provided a gracious unexplainable peace, as well as my ability to function. As the days wore on, Mom saw so many of God's people rise to the occasion, coming to offer food, services, and assistance. Impromptu circles of prayer often formed in the house. Throughout the funeral planning process and the funeral celebration itself, she watched, taking note of the help I received from my church friends, of the unnatural calm, of the laughter in my house as we recounted Jay's antics on the road, at home, and at work.

She stayed at the house for days after the funeral to guard the door, the phone, and the conversation. Observing. Listening. Watching. At first, her plan was to take me back to Wisconsin with her, but by the time we got Jay buried, she was making plans to move to Grand Rapids instead. It was obvious that I had a network in place that she couldn't replicate in Wisconsin.

I watched her during that time too. When, at the funeral, Pastor Ed offered an invitation to accept Jesus, I hoped that she would finally acknowledge her need of a Savior. She didn't. But she did concede that there was probably a God. She even went so far as to say she didn't think abortion should be legalized anymore. The issue she'd protested for, the right she'd fought for—a woman's right to choose—had turned in her mind into the right to an abusive form of birth control.

She went home to Wisconsin and we talked every day. She was my safe spot. We talked about Jake and Eli and what I was doing with the house renovations. When I started to freak out about the accumulating costs, she assured me that fixing the house and staying put was the right decision. We talked about the neighbors' comments and the women at church. We talked about Jay. We talked about the people who came over and who called. She celebrated the good moments of every day and listened to me snuffle at night. I told her how well my pillars were taking care of me and how Craig, the flaky pilot, was emailing me articles about widows who were bilked out of their life insurance by con artists, urging me to beware of people whose offers seemed too good to be true.

"Can't you come back for a visit?" I asked her. "I miss you and I want you to see what I'm doing to the house."

"How 'bout you and the boys fly here for Thanksgiving?"

"That would be good, but can't you come back now?" I pleaded.

"I really can't right now. You and those little boys come here."

"The boys would like that. I could tell them we're flying on one of Grandma G's puddle-jumpers."

"Right. It'll be great! I'll pick you up at the airport."

And she did, waving exuberantly at the terminal window. We had

Thanksgiving dinner (takeout from the deli, since she never cooked) at her house. The next day we drove to my brother Dion's house. While the children played in the next room, Mom, Dion, his wife, Lisa, and I sat in the comfy family room. A fire snapped and popped in the fireplace.

"Look at this picture of you, Robyn," said my brother, selecting a photo from the box Mom had brought along and handing it to me. It was a black-and-white of me as a six-year-old. I was smiling a toothless grin and my hair was unevenly cut. "Did you cut your own hair?" he asked.

"No, I did not!" I laughed, looking at Mom. "She did!"

"Not true. You cut it and I just fixed it."

"Doesn't look like anyone fixed it!" my brother said. "You sure were a homely kid."

"But look how I turned out! You got the brains, but I got the beauty."

"Where was that taken? Grandma Clark's?"

"I think so. Look at that gaudy wallpaper."

"She loved that stuff. It's even on the ceiling."

"Remember all the dishes she would get dirty for a holiday meal? Mountains of dishes!"

"Like you *ever* did dishes," I said, poking Dion.

"Women's work!"

We all laughed about how preposterously the gender-specific jobs had been divvied out for holidays. Men overate, then sat around watching ball games until they fell asleep or needed something more to eat. The men in my family were all hard workers, but not on holidays.

Mom sighed. "It's so good to have us all together."

We all watched the fire lick the logs. It was quiet, the kind of silence that comes with familiarity. The kind that comes with contentment. Mom spoke up again, in what was intended to be a lighthearted tone. "The cancer is back. My counts are all askew again."

We stared at her in disbelief. I started to cry. "No! How can that be? You went through so much already. The treatments were supposed to give you another five to ten years! It's only been a couple of months! What happened to your remission?"

"No one has a good answer for that. I'm really not sure what will happen now. Chemo again or maybe a bone marrow transplant. I meet with the doctors next week."

"Well, that sucks," spat Dion.

"It does suck. I agree. But I feel good and we're all together. Don't worry. Now, who's ready for another piece of Lisa's dessert? I know I am."

Sugar was my mother's antidote and addiction.

While doctors determined the next course of action, she sequestered herself in her condo, restricted visitors, and tried to stay as healthy as a dying woman can.

I never had a knack for decorating, not even for Christmas—Jay had always picked the tree and decorated the house—and that year, I definitely didn't have the heart for it. I planned to spend Christmas in Wisconsin, and since our house was being remodeled anyway, I painted a Christmas tree outline on the wall and Jake and Eli decorated it with markers and construction paper cutouts.

In February, Mom felt well enough and brave enough to visit! Yes, she still had cancer, but her counts had been stable since November. She didn't *feel* sick. She decided she was going to thoroughly engage in relationships for whatever time she had left. And who knew—she might have years. No one could say for sure. We made Valentine cards for the boys' classmates. We shopped for carpet and light fixtures. She rearranged my furniture, and we hardly slept at all, talking late into the night. We even thumbed our noses at fate, perusing homeschooling curriculum that she would use to homeschool my boys when she moved to Grand Rapids. We window shopped for condos near my house.

A week after she returned home, she was admitted to the hospital with a stubborn, unidentified infection. The cancer wasn't worsening, but the antibiotics didn't seem to be affecting the mysterious infection. I decided to leave the boys with friends and go to Wisconsin to stay with her.

I called Craig, who had visited us a few times since Jay's funeral. Once for a Packers game—he came laden with all manner of football snack food: Hot Pockets and pizza rollups, chips and pop, with not a vegetable in sight, of course. He came again to deliver regulation Packers helmets to Jake and Eli from his trip to the Super Bowl. The Packers had won the title. Another time he took us all to the movies. He always brought the party with him. He told the boys and me wonderful stories about their dad and their grandpa-with-the-big-belly.

He came to church with us, and the whispers started. When curious congregants asked about his intentions, he said, "I just want to do for Jay's kids what Andy did for me."

He'd insisted that if I needed a flight anywhere, he would be happy to take me. I had to admit, I was starting to warm up to this compassionate version of him. He was fun to be with and it was lovely to have the company of a man.

Craig wasn't the kind of pilot who wore a stiff uniform and shiny black wingtips. He flew small planes in and out of little airports all over the United States, and his uniform was a Hawaiian shirt, shorts, and tennis shoes. He was an accomplished pilot, and the bulk of his income came from teaching other free spirits to fly and from taking folks places they couldn't see or get to on airliners. Some wanted to see an aerial view of their home. Romantics soared over a mattress of clouds under a fully moonlit sky, artists viewed the color kaleidoscope of Midwest autumns, and dreamers captured two sunrises on the same morning, one from the air and one from the ground. Of course, there were times when someone just needed to get somewhere else.

Craig also worked as a waiter at a fine Italian restaurant. He called it an ATM job, because with his gregarious personality, he raked in the cash. During the school year, he drove a short bus outfitted for kids with special needs. Plus he operated a lawn-mowing service in the summer. He was busy, but flexible. Flexible enough that when I called to ask him to fly me to Madison, he came immediately.

I was pretty nervous about getting into his tiny airplane, which had no heat, to fly across Lake Michigan in the wintry blackness of night—especially after he told me I wouldn't last seven minutes in the cold water if anything went wrong. *Oh God,* I prayed, climbing in, *I do not want to leave my babies orphaned!*

After he got my suitcase stowed and my seat harness clicked into place, Craig was quiet most of the way. There wasn't much to talk about.

My mom was deathly ill and I wasn't entirely sure what could be done. The engine was loud, and it was easy to sink into my own thoughts as we glided under the wispy, cloud-covered moon.

I was frozen when we landed, in spite of the snowmobile suit Craig had dressed me in. He got me some hot chocolate at the terminal while he tied down the plane and secured a car to drive me to the hospital.

At the front door of the hospital, he unloaded my suitcase, gave me a hug, and said, "I'll be praying for you. Call me if you need anything."

I was startled by Mom's appearance when I entered her room. She was pale. Drawn. Her face was full of pain.

"I knew you'd come," she whispered when I walked into the hospital room. I smiled, thinking that she'd raised me to know that was the only and obvious thing to do. I sat with her that night and into the morning, willing the medicine to work. At midmorning, restless, I sneaked out for some sunlight. (She kept her room dark because the light hurt her eyes and caused headaches.) I went down the elevator and crossed the lobby toward the exit. To my shock, Craig was still in the lobby!

"What …what are you doing here?" I asked, incredulous.

"I thought I'd hang around. Pray. Be here if you needed anything."

I didn't know what to say. It was too much. I started to cry. He pulled me into his chest, hugging me. "The doctors don't know how to treat her. We just have to wait and hope for improvement. I just can't lose her now. I just can't."

He didn't say a thing. He just let me snot and slobber all over his shirt.

After what seemed like a long time, I wiped my eyes and nose. Self-consciously, I looked around the busy lobby. "Well, thanks for staying, but there's no telling how long I'll be. Just go home. I'll call you if there's any change."

I went back to Mom's room. A small light was on, and she was sitting up, a tiny bit of color flushing her cheeks. New hope trickled in.

The hope was contagious. Doctors, their faces relieved, started making eye contact with me again as they talked about treatment. Protocols to attack the sickness were discussed with a new sense of confidence.

New orders for scans, blood tests, bone marrow draws, and consultations were given.

For the next two days, we had a gay old time. We talked about Jake and Eli—about what a good idea it was for me to have them. "See! If I hadn't nagged at you to have children before your eggs petrified, where would you be?"

"You're right. They're great!"

"And smart."

"Well, of course they are."

Naturally, she took all the credit. "They get that from me."

"Where should they go to school until you move to Grand Rapids to homeschool them?"

She laughed. "They're such clever boys; you'll have to urge the teachers to stay sharp till I get there."

I told her about Craig's visits and his camping in the lobby of the hospital. "You think he's interested in me? It's kinda soon to be thinking about a boyfriend, but he's so much fun and seems so invested in us."

Mom never missed a beat. "Just sleep with him. Get it out of your system. He's a grasshopper. You're an ant."

"You're a big help."

"I am, actually."

Though it was all written down, she reviewed the arrangements she wanted for her funeral. "You can have the memorial service and funeral at Hamre's in Lodi. Take everyone down to the café on Main Street for lunch." She twinkled a smile. "There's plenty of money for that." She'd settled the lawsuit against the construction company that dropped the flagpole on her head for $300,000. "I want to be cremated and buried in the family plot on the hill next to my brother, Lon. I've drawn the sculpture I want for a marker. It's in the folder with all my important documents."

"What do I say at your funeral, Mom? Funerals are supposed to give comfort and hope to the living. Do we have a minister or official? Who talks?"

"I don't know, Rob," she said.

"You know—when Jay died, I'm sure he went straight to heaven. In heaven, there are mansions prepared for new arrivals. There are no tears, no sickness, and everyone gets new bodies. It's a place of great beauty and joy—a wonderful place, Mama," I told her. "I want us all to be there together."

"Sounds good to me," she said.

"But Jesus is the only gateway for a sinful person to get to a holy God in heaven."

Her response startled me: "I don't have a problem with that."

While it wasn't exactly a profession of her faith in God, it was closer to it than anything I'd ever heard her say. I was ecstatic.

By the end of that day, her condition had improved so significantly that plans to release her were made and a bone marrow transplant was planned. "We'll release her tomorrow," I was told. "At home, she'll need to rest up for another round of chemotherapy."

We had a plan. Order was coagulating in the midst of chaos.

The next day started out filled with expectation. Mom's regular nurse intercepted me in the hall before I got to her room. She spoke softly, apologetically. "Robyn, your mom had a bad night. The medicine she's been taking to battle the infection is so strong … her lungs have hemorrhaged. She's going to die today. You should call your brother and get him here as quickly as possible. I'm so sorry."

I was paralyzed. She was only sixty-one! I wasn't ready for my mom to die. But most importantly, my mom wasn't ready to die. Without faith in Jesus, she would be eternally separated from God. I would never see her again!

I frantically reminded God about my prayers for her to see him, to be touched by him.

He answered: *It's you, Robyn.*

We had come down to the final hours and *I* was the someone in her path she trusted enough to listen to. I was the case study in a *dramatically* changed lifestyle as a result of accepting Christ. God had revealed his love and mercy to her by placing her in my home the weekend my husband died.

I walked into Mom's room. She looked up at me and shook her head sorrowfully.

Our faces contorted in that way that happens when you try to talk but you know you're going to gut-cry. Disbelief. Denial. Disappointment. I missed her already.

I wasn't sure what to say. "Mom, you can't wait any longer. You have to decide now. You need to call on Jesus as your Savior. I can't stand the idea of getting to heaven and not finding you there. You have to receive Jesus' gift of salvation! You have to believe there is a God in heaven who loves you. But he's holy and he can't tolerate the presence of sin. The only way for a sinful person to have access to him is by accepting that Jesus died to pay the penalty for your sins and rose again. Then you have assurance of eternal life with him in heaven!"

She paused just for a second, then in her inimitable style, she responded with an abrupt, "Well, don't you have enough pull to get me in?"

Under different circumstances, I might have laughed out loud, but this was life and death—*eternal* life and death. I smiled and tried to explain gently again how accepting Jesus as Savior is a personal decision. "No one can inherit salvation, any more than you can be good enough to offset the bad on some cosmic balance sheet and get into heaven on merit. It all comes down to receiving Jesus' death and resurrection in faith."

As usual, she countered with an objection, but less confrontational this time. As though she were resigned to her fate. "Robyn, I don't have the kind of faith you do, and I don't have time to get it."

So true. "I've been following Jesus for seven years already," I said. "My faith has had time to grow. But if you have a mustard seed–size piece of faith that what I am telling you is true, that would be enough."

The verse that rushed into my mind was Romans 10:9: "If you declare with your mouth, 'Jesus is Lord,' and believe in your heart that God raised him from the dead, you will be saved." I wanted to know that she believed it—and I wanted to hear her say it.

"Can you do that, Mama? Do you believe with a mustard seed–size piece of faith that what I am telling you is true?"

"Yes," she said. "That much I can do. I want the peace."

Thank you, Father God.

I called my brother, Dion, who lived several hours away. While we waited for him to arrive, there was very little talking and intermittent sobbing. This was worse than dreadful. Even if I could have taken her place, she never would have let me. She gave everything to the people she loved, and she loved my brother and me most of all.

Two of her friends had fallen on hard times. Without time to amend her will, she asked me to write checks out to them. My hand was shaking so badly that I had to do one of them over. My mind couldn't remember how to make out a simple check.

Dion arrived early that afternoon, calm but obviously distraught. We asked the doctors about transplants, new medications—any treatment that might reverse Mom's death sentence.

They offered no hope.

All the time Dion was with us, Mom told him nothing about her decision to accept Jesus as Savior—nothing about having a fresh peace or being on her way to heaven. Why was that—was she simply preoccupied with trying to stay alive?

Nor did I say anything. That must be what temporary insanity is like—not acting in a way that is consistent with your nature. Why it never occurred to me to confirm her salvation experience in front of Dion, a non-believer, will forever be a mystery to me.

And it's a shame. No one on the planet had the influence on Dion that Mom did, and once she died, there was no way to prove that I wasn't making it all up to coerce him into making a similar decision. Nor could I prove that she hadn't just told me what I needed to hear out of love for me, so that I would be able to process my grief. "Always be prepared to give an answer to everyone who asks you to give the reason for the hope that you have," my Bible says in 1 Peter 3:15. I dearly wish I had. I so wish Dion could know what she said to me. If I had any day of my life to live over differently, it is that day.

Dion and I stayed with Mom all day and into the night. Nurses and doctors kept coming in to check on her, saying the end was nearer. I left for a bit so that Dion could have time alone with her.

By the time I returned, Mom had slipped into a coma. She died the next morning.

◈

I was tortured for years after her death about whether she had said—and meant—the right thing that final day. Was I just fooling myself? Did she really believe what she said, or was she just saying it to give me peace? I hated that we had missed the opportunity to have my precious, smart brother hear about Jesus from her mouth. I have often had to remind myself: It isn't my responsibility to save anyone, not even my mom and brother. The enemy knows how weak I am and how desperately I want to know that she is safe in heaven with God Almighty. And yet I can't *know* that—I can only *trust* that it is well with her soul. God has repeatedly reminded me that my part was merely to live out, in front of her, his gift of salvation to me. To tell her and others about Jesus' gift of eternal life. To offer comfort to her in her valley of the shadow of death. I sincerely hope that she will be on the welcoming committee when I reach heaven's gate.

◈

I hated being left behind. Again. Grieving another loss. Weary of being the one still alive to clean up the mess. More phone calls and letters to family members and friends: "I just thought you should know that Mom died yesterday, and her funeral is next Wednesday. Yes, I'm sorry too. I know you'll miss her." When everyone else has been comforted and fed at the funeral, and when the grave is dug and covered back up again, I will be left in a world without a husband—and now without my mother.

Craig flew me back to Michigan so I could collect the boys and return by car for the funeral. He stayed with me like an old dog, hovering on the periphery. He stayed through the funeral, waited in countless reception areas as I met with lawyers and doctors and neighbors and relatives. Then he packed me up and took me and the boys home. I have no idea where he slept, or even whether he ate. I just remember that he was everywhere I was: at the funeral, at the diner for the receptions, at the gravesite ... snapping pictures.

Mom's funeral was held at the funeral parlor because she had no church affiliation, and Dion adamantly refused to have any reference to God in the service. The absolute best part of the funeral and the weeks that followed were the words spoken about Mom, and the letters and cards I received from her friends. Men and women from all over the country conveyed their sympathy and wrote lengthy descriptions of how they remembered my beautiful, brilliant, best-in-the-world mother:

"She was extraordinary."

"Ahead of her time."

"She was respected among her peers and beloved by her students."

"She will be remembered well."

"The world is indeed a better place because of the work she did here."

Mom had made the process of sorting through her personal effects as easy as she could. She had marked and designated what art and jewelry pieces were to be given to whom. She had burned her journals and sorted the family photos. Thankfully, Dion, an attorney, handled all the legalities of selling her sporty convertible and her condo and arranging for the custom tombstone she'd designed.

On the outside I am strong. In a crisis, I make the calls and the meals and the day-to-day decisions. Then suddenly, a tidal wave of grief picks me up and throws me about, and I cry out. "God," I ask, "what's next? My children? Will the house burn down? Please just take me next. I can't bear any more loss. Let me catch my breath, please."

Despite those heart cries, I am confident of this: God is with me; God does not make mistakes; God has a plan for my life; God keeps his promises. I feel like a tike on a two-wheeler without training wheels. It's the first time out of the garage in the spring, the year after I first learned to ride. I know how, and I know the bike will hold me, but I'm wobbly and I need to keep my eyes on where I want to go. If I stare at the pavement in front of my tire, I will surely crash. Instead, I need to keep my eyes on my destination.

People watch you during a trial. It's like watching ocean waves crash or a fire burn. They are drawn by an inexplicable curiosity. When, during that trial, you lift your hands and sing his praises, when you say out loud that Jesus Christ is your King—people take note. When your life falls apart, they put you under a microscope to see how big your God really is.

My mom watched. It's no accident that she was there when Jay died. Did Jay have to die in front of my mother for her to accept Jesus? Nope. But, did God use those events to draw her to him? I believe he did.

Chapter 12

LEARNING
TO FLY

As much as I didn't want to be in a world without Jay, I was. As much as I don't want to be in a world without Mom, I am. It's often lonely and sometimes scary.

As a suddenly single mom, my days were full of kids and school papers, grocery shopping and housework. There were no grandmas to help out, no ex-husband to conveniently take the children for an evening or a weekend. It was all me, all the time. I adjusted to being alone even while I was surrounded by people.

I was impatient for "next" to escape "now." The next day. The next house project. The next trip. The next friend stopping by. The next diversion. The next husband?

I was uneasy about actually dating. I was afraid of being judged. Afraid that people would think my marriage to Jay hadn't been good. Or that I hadn't really loved Jay. That I was being foolish. That it was too soon. That any suitor was only trying to get into my knickers or my bank account. I was afraid I'd end up on television's *Unsolved Mysteries* show. Afraid my little boys would be orphaned. Afraid they'd live with distant relatives and survive on carryout and SpaghettiOs. Afraid their clothes would never get ironed. Afraid they'd forget all about me.

Craig visited us several times that winter. I tried to look at him as just another friend of the family, but after Mom's death, I found myself eagerly anticipating his next visit. He'd been stalwart and kind, generous and available throughout the aftermath of her death.

Knowing Craig's family history was reassuring. He'd been raised in a well-to-do family anchored in Christian traditions and training. His parents had been one of ten couples that grew a tiny church plant in a coffee shop into the megachurch of Elmbrook in Milwaukee, Wisconsin. His dad was on the search committee that brought renowned speakers and authors Stuart and Jill Briscoe from England to serve as pastors.

Craig was very different from Jay. He'd grown up on tennis courts and golf courses, not football fields. He had never been in a fistfight or raced cars for pink slips; he didn't know how to use a variable-speed drill. He didn't smoke or drink or use drugs and never had.

I was intrigued, ready to tiptoe into the dating scene for the first time in sixteen years. Craig had great credentials. He had no bad habits. He was so fun. And handsome.

On one of his visits, we had the talk. Craig called it the Great Awakening.

I started. "I really enjoy our time together."

"Yeah, I like spending time with you too."

"It's comforting to spend time with someone who knew Jay and his family. You have such great memories and tell wonderful stories about them."

"I'm just trying to pay back all that Andy and his family did for me."

"That is so magnanimous. I really appreciate it."

"Well, it's not as if I'd been doing anything special with my life. It feels good to give back."

"Uhm, you know, I think I should let you know I'm not going to be single forever. I hope to marry again."

"I would think so. When you start to feel better—you know, get past some of the grief—you'll find someone. He'll be a lucky man."

"Do you ever think about playing a larger role in our lives?"

"Who, me? No! I would never presume. I've had all the chances I deserve. More, probably."

"Well, we seem to get along well. The boys love you. I could see us spending more time together. In an exclusive relationship. If you're interested."

There was a pause before he answered. With a sincerity that couldn't be faked, he said, "I never dreamed you would be interested in me. Yes! I would be honored to be part of your lives."

I paused. "There is a stipulation. I'm not jeopardizing my health or orphaning my kids because I get AIDS. I have no idea where you've been in your travels or with whom you have spent your time—or with whom your partners have spent their time. If you want any of *this, ever*, you'll have to be tested now and again in six months (the incubation time for AIDS to show up), during which time you'll have to be celibate."

Documentation pronouncing a clean bill of health was presented the next visit. Craig got down on one knee and said, "Robyn, I feel like God is giving me another chance. I've made a mess of my life, and I don't deserve another opportunity—but if you find me worthy, I will love you for the rest of my life. My dying thought will be of you."

We were officially a couple.

Craig quit his jobs in Wisconsin and moved to Grand Rapids eight months after Jay died so we could spend more time together. After all, it's hard to get to know someone well if you only spend a day or two at a time with them. He rented a room from a divorced man looking for some extra income and a little company in his empty house. It was June, and we had the whole summer to fritter away. Craig lived on his savings during our summer romp and planned to find work when the boys went back to school in the fall, duplicating the hodgepodge of jobs he'd left in Wisconsin.

Before Craig moved to Grand Rapids, I thought I'd be alone forever. That I'd had the best of life already. But with Craig, I started a whole new exciting adventure. He took us to ball games and musicals. We ate elephant ears at carnivals and rode on elephants at the circus. We drove with the windows wide open and the Jock Jams blaring. He flew us to resorts with indoor/outdoor pools and scrumptious buffet lines. We cheered for the Red Knight while eating like Vikings at the Medieval Times Dinner & Tournament theater. Taking vacations was new to the children and me, but Craig was full of ideas. His family had taken annual six-week vacations in Europe, Asia, and the Middle East. I had never even seen an ocean! Craig had a long track record of business ventures in his wake, one of which was a dance studio. He'd even competed on an amateur level for a time. I bought fancy dresses for the first time since my wedding to Jay—long flowing ones, short sexy ones. We went ballroom dancing in elegant attire, twirling around the floor like something out of a Disney movie.

Craig had been raised in a big house with a swimming pool in the basement. He'd spent his weekends at the country club—but when his dad died, the money died too. Although Craig was no longer wealthy, his stories and our excursions created the illusion of affluence to my neighbors, friends, and church onlookers, and I did not correct that illusion.

There were a few raised eyebrows about Craig's three divorces. But since Craig was going to be my third husband, the fact that I was going to be his fourth wife didn't really rattle me. When my brother expressed concerns, I said, "I'm keeping my money and my body separated from Craig until I know he's trustworthy." Good intentions. I wish I'd followed through.

Craig told me that before we could make any firm wedding plans, he needed to settle a $10,000 debt from a joint business venture with his ex-girlfriend. I didn't want him to have any more contact with her, so I insisted that he let me pay off the loan. He agreed reluctantly. I reasoned that if I had the debt and he had the money, I would want him to expedite our future together.

We spent all our time together, sometimes with the children and other times on dates without the boys. Jake and Eli enjoyed the activities. Craig was spontaneous and full of unpredictable surprises. I was happy and that spilled over on them. Everyone was all smiles. Craig made me feel so special—showering me with compliments, taking me out in pretty dresses. I melted into him. And not just on the dance floor. While I didn't have a ring or a date, I knew we were going to get married. We started sleeping together. I told myself it was the natural course of things. And it felt so good in the moment, like warm cookies and cold milk. Why wait?

I was so hungry to be connected with someone again. But afterward, I was filled with remorse and guilt. I was embarrassed and ashamed—but I couldn't stop. I didn't stop. I pushed to set a wedding date to legitimize my actions. I didn't want to be "that girl" again. That girl who sleeps around. That girl without standards. That girl whose testimony about God's sufficient power to avoid temptation has been corrupted.

In fall, instead of looking for work, Craig enrolled at the School of Missionary Aviation Technology to learn to be an airframe and power plant mechanic. I told him I would pay for his tuition and his living expenses so he could focus his full attention on his studies—and on me.

I could afford it. Jay and I had been debt free when he died, and we had lived on a pretty austere budget to make that happen. Suddenly, I had more money than I'd ever dreamed of. Even after all the home renovations, I had a chunk of life insurance remaining. As Jay's widow I would get Social Security until the youngest child turned sixteen or I remarried. Plus I was getting almost $2,000 a month from my mom's pension and the lawsuit settlement. I would continue to get those checks for about three years, enough time for Craig to graduate, build a clientele, and begin to support us. He was already a certified flight instructor. With an A&P license he could work at any of the airports in and around Grand Rapids, fixing airplanes and using his airplane to offer flight lessons.

I was ready to be married again. Ready for the boys to have a dad again. I didn't want to raise them without a father. Who would ready them for manhood? Who was going to wrestle with them? Teach them to catch a ball? Backflip off the diving board? Craig insisted that it would be an honor to help raise Jay's boys. He had never wanted children of his own, so he'd had a vasectomy at twenty-four. Instead of seeing that as a red flag, I was relieved. My proverbial quiver was full. I had two beautiful, well-behaved, intelligent boys. I didn't want more. I had heard nothing but horror stories about blended families and was worried about what my boys would have to adjust to if we added an "our" child.

As much as people wanted me to feel better and to be better so *they* could feel better, there is something about change that grates people. It was hardest for Jay's family. To them, it seemed disloyal for me to be moving on. They'd hoped the boys would carry on their dad's name as the last of the Andraszczyk clan. Craig and I agreed that it was important for the children to remember Jay, but I wanted more than that. I wanted us to be a family. To all have the same last name. I wanted Craig to adopt the children. I legally changed the boys' last name to Treu the day Craig and I got married, but we'd have to wait a year before we could file for adoption. All of Jay's pictures remained on the walls and in wallets. Craig and I regaled the boys with stories of Jay's childhood, his adolescence, and how he embraced fatherhood. But his memory was all we could hold on to. He wasn't coming back, and the rest of us had to keep moving forward.

Craig and I decided to get married in a month that contained neither of our birthdays, no previous wedding anniversary, and no anniversary of the day we had buried someone important. That left January. He asked if I wanted a diamond engagement ring. I did want a diamond—a *big* diamond. I wanted a diamond so big it would be dangerous to swim with for fear it would sink me in the pool. The classy thing, he insisted, would be to buy the best quality, clarity, and color, and forget about size. Snob. In the end, we settled on a nearly flawless 1.25 carat, marquis-cut diamond. We bought it three weeks before the wedding with my life insurance money.

"What are you thinking about for a honeymoon?" Craig asked. "Want to go anywhere special?" Craig wanted to show me all the places I had never seen, which was everywhere outside the Midwest. When he traveled, he chose a destination that sounded interesting and headed that direction, but if he found something more fascinating along the way, he just changed his plans. I knew that he had been everywhere, and I wanted to *appear* adventurous—but the most exotic place I felt comfortable going was two hours north, to the resort town of Traverse City, Michigan.

Craig scoffed. "Traverse City? Traverse City! We're not going to Traverse City for our honeymoon. We'll go to … Europe! We'll go skiing in the Alps."

That did not sound good to me at all. I'd tried skiing once. I couldn't stand, stop, get on the chairlift, or use the rope tow. It had been an utter disaster that became a family joke for years. "But I don't know how to ski!" I said. Craig's response? "The Alps are a great place to learn."

We set a wedding date. January 2, 1998. The same pastor who'd buried Jay would officiate my wedding to Craig. We got married with all of thirty people in attendance and just one attendant—mine. Craig's best man had died in a plane crash a few weeks before the wedding. If I was superstitious, I might have thought it a warning sign.

Without attendants or ushers, Craig and I greeted attendees. He was barefoot, wearing a white tux and John Lennon sunglasses. I wore stiletto heels and a black disposable dress—short, fitted, and black-beaded. It couldn't be washed or dry cleaned, so I calculated that if I didn't go jogging in it, I could use it for about sixteen hours before I had to throw it away.

When everyone was seated, Craig changed into a black tux and I put on an elegant cream-colored gown for the ceremony. Before we walked down the aisle of the chapel to exchange vows, Craig pulled me aside and said, "Babelicious, you can do better than me. If you have any second thoughts before we do this, I understand. I'm the one getting the best part of this marriage. You don't have to go through with it. We can still have the party downtown and no hard feelings. I just wanted you to know there is still time to change your mind."

I thought, *Isn't he wonderful?*

There was no hesitation for me. I thought that was the most wonderful way to say *I love you.*

We walked down the aisle together. My only regret was that my mom wasn't there to see it.

Craig's idea of planning the honeymoon trip was to buy two round-trip tickets to Frankfurt, Germany, rent a car, and see what looked interesting along the road. It was unseasonably warm in the Alps that year, so Craig declared that the skiing would be lousy and altered our plans. Instead of being hurled down a mountain, we ended up in Paris, France. He took me to all the sights: the Arc de Triomphe, the Louvre, Notre Dame Cathedral, and the Eiffel Tower. We drove the Autobahn. I ate divine cuisine. I walked ancient halls. I viewed treasured art. I was captivated. Craig was amused by my awe.

It felt Bohemian. Far from home. No responsibility. Eat what you want. Sleep as late as you like. Wander the streets. Ponder the history. Admire the beauty.

※

When we got home from Europe, Craig moved his things into my house. Boxes of artifacts from his various travels, a piano for the living room, Franklin Mint figurines for the curio. A television in our bedroom.

"Why do we need a TV in the bedroom?"

"I like to sleep with the TV on."

"Ugh. All night?"

"All night."

"Okay, I guess we can try that."

The volume fluctuations and the flashing of light at a scene change were beyond disruptive. My sleep was constantly interrupted.

It didn't take very long for me to discover the other reason he wanted a television in the bedroom. He liked to watch porn. He had boxes of videos he wanted to share with me.

In addition to his various collections, Craig came with an airplane, a motorcycle, and riding lawnmowers, which now also belonged to me. He announced, "It's ridiculous to own a vehicle that you don't know how to operate." His plan was to teach me first to fly the airplane and then to ride motorcycles, all of which sounded very exciting. But when he started looking at the riding lawnmower, I said that I had learned enough.

There is truth in the old adage *A husband should not attempt to teach his wife to drive. Driving lessons are a lot cheaper than a divorce.* Learning to fly was horribly hard for me; all the technical, weather-related, and directional stuff vexed me. Craig had no patience for my ineptness and was constantly shouting at me. To top it off, my own flying made me sick. I swallowed little pieces of Dramamine the first forty hours of my training.

After months of lessons, I quit. "I like being a passenger. You fly us."

"You said you'd get your license. I believed you."

"I changed my mind. It was a dumb idea."

"So you lied."

"I changed my mind."

"What else are you going to change your mind about? Being married to me?"

"That's ridiculous. I just don't want to learn to fly an airplane."

"Obviously, I can't trust anything you say."

"You can't trust anything I say because I changed my mind about learning to fly? That's absurd!"

"It's not. Your word is your word. If you don't get your pilot's license, I can't trust you on any level."

I was confused. Not trust me? Where did that come from? It wasn't enough that I subsidized his tuition, added his name to all my bank accounts and the title to the house, and changed the children's last name to his? Still a newlywed and wanting peace in the house, I caved. "Fine. I'll get my pilot's license so you can trust me. But I want a different instructor."

Craig agreed. Within a month, I'd aced the written test, which had never been an issue. (I am a great pilot on paper.) When I took the flight test, I nailed the oral exam, and my flight was the best ever. Not the best ever in the history of the world, but *my* best ever. My stalls and maneuvers were spot on. My grass landing was so soft, we didn't even feel the touchdown. Never had another landing like that.

I was a licensed pilot.

When we landed, Craig walked out to the field and asked the state flight examiner if I had passed.

"She did," the examiner said. "In fact, she did well."

Craig's response: "Well, okay, I know she doesn't suck, but really—how bad was it?"

"Really, she did very well. She's a good pilot."

When the examiner left, I asked Craig, "What was all that about? You heard him. Do you take pride in embarrassing me?"

He said, "I knew you'd pass. I wanted you to hear the examiner tell me how good it was."

It wasn't the only time Craig's manner of communication was startling. One night we ran into our pastor's wife out celebrating her birthday. Craig said, "Happy birthday. I know it's rude to ask how old you are, so … how much do you weigh?"

If someone asked how we met, he'd bend toward the inquirer and whisper conspiratorially, "She used to be married to my best friend. The trick was making it look like an accident." I got used to smiling and shaking my head in playful participation. You either loved him or loathed him.

I never loved flying, but I did love saying that I could. I took some trips alone, I flew the kids across Lake Michigan to visit my family, and we took some day trips to Mackinac Island. It was never pleasurable. Most of the time, I thought it would have made more sense to use the car. By the time you drive to the airport, fuel up and do the pre-flight inspection, navigate to the destination, land, taxi, tie-down, find ground transportation, and get to the final destination, you could have driven for about the same amount of time and less money. For long-distance trips, it was easier and more economical to fly commercial.

After getting my pilot's license, the motorcycle endorsement was easy. I took a weekend class and was riding with Eli as a passenger the next Saturday. There is no sensation of speed in a plane, but on a motorcycle the wind crashes across exposed skin and blows your hair back. The engine noise and the wind blowing by your ears preclude conversation, and thoughts run free without the distraction of the radio or telephone or human voice. Eli sat on the back of my bike, pretending to be Spider-man, shooting webs from his wrists or flapping his arms like a bird.

Craig was terrific at dating, weddings, and high days state occasions. He noticed every nail color change, new dress, and haircut. He made a big production out of every birthday and anniversary. Cards the entire week before—in the kitchen cupboard, in my bathrobe pocket, under my pillow, even in the mailbox. He bought flowers and rented yard signs. He celebrated my wedding anniversary to Jay with as much enthusiasm as our own. It was a great opportunity to tell his story of redemptive altruism—how by just trying to do the noble but selfless thing, he'd ended up with a trophy wife and the big house on the hill. It was over the top. It was our fairy tale, and he spun the story brilliantly.

At home it became a different story. Craig's transition to fathering was not smooth. He didn't have any experience parenting, and his expectations of the boys were beyond their skill set, age, or maturity. I had very well-behaved boys, but by our first anniversary, he was yelling, pushing, and punishing the boys for what seemed to me like minor infractions. It was unsettling. How long would it take him to get the hang of this?

In blended families, there is a tension between the biological parent's protective reflex and recognizing when the kids need correction. How long should I wait for him to learn, to soften, to have realistic expectations? Who from outside the family could I ask for advice and perspective without violating marital trust?

Hard questions. In the meantime, I justified Craig's treatment by telling myself and the children that he just needed some time to get into our routine. I made excuses to babysitters when they asked about the way Craig talked to the children or about comments the boys had made about his sanctions.

Sometimes we all got along well. I hoped and prayed those times would become the norm. God is big enough to undo a little damage, right?

⚬❧⚬

We'd been married about eighteen months when, getting the kids ready for bed one night, I was horrified to see big, dark, purple bruises on their backsides.

"What happened with the kids?" I demanded of Craig.

"I spanked them for not putting the toilet seat down. I have told them before, and they're too stupid to remember, so I spanked them. They have to be reminded about everything. Maybe this will help their memory."

I was incredulous. It was one thing to smash toys with a sledgehammer that hadn't been put away in a timely manner or cut up their stuffed animals with shears for C's on a report card, but this was more than I could allow.

"You can't do that," I said. "It's too much! It constitutes physical abuse, and I won't tolerate it. If an authority at school saw bruising like that, Child Protective Services would be alerted. I won't risk having the boys taken from me because of how you choose to discipline them!"

Craig rationalized. "It's for their own good. They have to learn to listen. It doesn't hurt them; it's just a spanking with a paddle. My dad walloped me with a belt till I bled. I missed days of school because I couldn't walk! Today, I'm thankful for his discipline."

"That's wrong, Craig! You can't discipline our children like that! Ever!"

He didn't spank them again. But at home, he often berated them with insults and belittling remarks. When one of the boys was learning to tie a necktie, Craig had him stand in front of a mirror to try it. When his little fingers fumbled with the knot, Craig slapped at his head and hands. "Are you stupid? Are you an idiot? Who can't tie a tie? It's not hard!"

My heart broke. How long should I let this go on? I was in turmoil. How much should I allow? Were the boys being abused? Whom could I tell? What would I say? Was I complicit?

The more I pleaded for softness, the more demanding he became to counteract me. He said he had to be firmer so that the children wouldn't become spoiled.

From the outside, our lives looked storybook perfect, but inside, the walls were crumbling. I banned the porn from our sex lives, but he carried on without me. We argued about the children and about money. My Social Security had stopped when we married, and there were only a few more payments from my mom's pension fund left. The few students he had and the occasional mechanic jobs he got at the airport didn't even cover his personal expenses every month. One of us was going to have to go to work for real. I thought it should be him.

I wanted to be home with my children. I liked being a mom and a homemaker. It had never been my intention to work outside the home. Jay and I had agreed that I would stay home indefinitely. It was my choice. My desire. I'd grown up watching my mom work full-time while going to school and raising her kids, and it was no life I wanted.

I asked my mom once if she was disappointed with the life choices I had made. After all, she was a PhD and my brother was an attorney. I was a housewife. She looked straight at me and said, "What you do here is more important than the value our society puts on educational credentialing. My generation fought for women's rights so that you could have choices. Don't let anyone take that away from you, Robyn. You are a terrific mom and wife. I am very proud of you."

Having her approval, even her endorsement, was cathartic. I am so glad I have the right to education and to vote and to work in the marketplace and to serve my country in the armed forces—but those things are a choice, not a requirement. I am not letting the female gender down if I choose to use my talents at home, for a season or for a lifetime.

I thought if Craig had a job or career that would give him some satisfaction he would be less controlling and critical at home. He manufactured all sorts of excuses not to work, but the truth was, he liked the persona he'd created. He didn't want to be a waiter or a mechanic around men who ran their own companies or had executive positions. He didn't want to manicure someone else's lawn.

"There isn't any work to be found! You try it if you think it's so easy."

"There's lots of work, just like what you did in Wisconsin. You just don't want to do it!"

"If you insist that I work, I'll have to go back to Wisconsin. Is that what you want?"

"Well, if that's your only choice, then I guess that's what you'll have to do."

He angrily threw some clothes into his car and tore out of the driveway. I locked the door and sighed with relief.

Three hours later he was back.

As much to keep the peace as to help him carry the financial burden, I took a part-time job working the front desk of a dental office. I thought he'd be relieved, maybe even encouraged. After all, I was doing everything he asked of me—certainly as much or more than he was.

He was neither relieved nor encouraged. "That job won't support us. It's a joke," he sneered.

It was obvious that Craig didn't want a job—he just wanted to be rich again. What better way than a get-rich-quick scheme? We went to an expensive seminar to learn day-trading on the stock market. It looked like gambling to me, and I didn't want anything to do with it. I tried it using Monopoly money for two weeks—and found that there was no way to predict the market trends with any consistency.

"I think there's a reason guys go to school to learn financial trends and need licenses to make trades," I said. "It makes no sense to me. I can't tolerate the risk. It's not for me."

"Are you content to work for some rich dentist, making all the money for him?"

"I don't really want to work outside the house at all. I'm perfectly happy taking care of the children, the house, and you. If you want to try this, fine, but I don't like it and I don't want to be tethered to a computer screen all day."

We agreed he would take $10,000 of the remaining life insurance money to see if he could make a go of day-trading. Before long, he insisted that he needed more—he couldn't make the trades he needed to build wealth with such a small amount. He needed, he said, at least $100,000! Again, to keep the peace and to give him a chance to win at something, I agreed.

He wasn't very good at day-trading either. He had a lot more losses than gains. Losing made him surly. I prayed that he would either swallow his pride and get a combination of jobs that would keep him busy and entertained while they provided an income or get serious about a career path—in aviation or elsewhere. He had the training and experience to pursue careers with commercial airlines or do corporate piloting. He did neither.

I prayed that given enough time and grace, smothered in love, perhaps Craig would surrender wholeheartedly to being a family man. To be a consistently good-natured person in the house as well as in public.

We'd been married just shy of two years when the notification arrived that our adoption case was to be heard. By then, I had developed a long list of reservations about giving Craig any legal claim on the kids. Losing money was one thing; I could recover from that. If we divorced, he was just as likely to fight for the kids out of spite as he was to walk away.

I didn't know what to do. If I balked, it would send him into a rage. If I went through with the adoption and he remained obstreperous, I might have to fight for my own children in a custody suit.

I labored with the decision. I knew that when Craig got his way, we often experienced a season of cheer, alacrity, and charm. I thought maybe this was another test to see if I was really dedicated to him. As harsh as he was at times, there were many other times when he was loving and kind. When it was bad, it always got better. Maybe if he was their "real dad" he would be less inclined to contend so vehemently for position.

What I knew of marriage was that the first years were hard. Wretchedly hard at first, then better, and finally, hopefully, good. As an optimist, I hoped he would change. That our marriage would evolve into a good thing, like the one I'd had with Jay. As a follower of Jesus, I knew nothing was impossible. My faith dared to trust that Craig would remember that he had promised to honor God with his life. I reasoned that we are all works in progress. When Craig was reading his Bible, participating at church, working productively, then life was wonderful.

I decided not to fear the worst and expect the best. To keep my agreement. To give Craig the benefit of the doubt. To trust him and trust God to stop the proceedings if it was the wrong choice. I was sure it was just a matter of time before Craig and I would have the marriage I dreamed of and thought it could start with the adoption.

Chapter 13

CRASH LANDING

There really wasn't much change immediately after the adoption. Craig still had mood swings and unexpected reactions to benign events. Sometimes he was all in. But increasingly, he simply disengaged. Became indifferent to everything. He ate, slept, and watched television. He gained weight. He paid little attention even to the day-trading. He sighed, "I wish you had known me when I wasn't a failure."

Me too, I thought.

I think he concluded that our marriage was destined to fail just like all his others. He didn't know how to make relationships work. He didn't like being a father. He didn't find satisfaction in his "work." It was as if he tried to create fullness or satisfaction from circumstances, and when those circumstances fell short, he fell into a depression. He tried to snap out of it by looking for ways to be around people he could entertain, if not impress. He looked for new adventure, new stories, new people. In short, he ran.

He volunteered to spend a month flying Billy, an evangelist friend, around New England for his speaking engagements. He came home a new man—calm, jovial, loving.

"Everywhere we went, people turned to Jesus," he said. "We went from one event to another—high schools, prisons, and camps. No preparation, just straight from the heart about who Billy used to be and how God healed him."

"Sounds like it was time well invested. You seem like your old self again. Do you want to do more of this?"

"I don't know. I just want to be in the center of all that. You ever think of writing a book? Maybe going on the road?"

I had written articles for moms' magazines and the church newsletter. But I wasn't sure I could write a book.

"Just tell your story," he urged me.

"I wouldn't know where to start, Craig. And while you love being married to an ex-Playboy Bunny who still fits into her costume, I'm not sure I want to expose my past to the world at large."

"Then I'll write it. I'll tell your story and our story."

Before I could decide whether the book tour was a God idea or just another way to avoid a traditional job, he was off again, this time to Florida to meet up with some folks from church at the SUN 'n FUN air show. While there, they asked Craig to look over a plane they ended up purchasing. Every phone call and postcard gushed with love.

> For 23 years after my dad died I waited for an answer to a prayer. My question and prayer request, "Lord, give me a reason to live. Show me how to do more than just go through the motions, teach me to live." Through all the wait there was comfort but his answer came when he made me part of this family.
>
> I'm in love with you, Robyn,
> Craig

When Craig came home, the reality that he would never again be part of a world where you take a little vacation and end up buying an airplane or two sank him.

"Why do these kids make so much noise when they eat?"

"Are you using paper napkins? You should live in a trailer. Maybe I'll buy one and put it in the backyard. You can live there till you can figure out how to set a table properly."

"You spend too much money!" says the guy traipsing all over the country in his personal aircraft.

And then, he was gone again. He registered to bicycle the RAGBRAI, Register's Annual Great Bicycle Ride Across Iowa. It isn't a race—it's the oldest, largest, and longest bicycle touring event in the world—a seven-day bicycle ride of 472 miles across the state of Iowa. Craig borrowed a bike but didn't train or buy special gear. He just took off. I thought he'd die of exhaustion or get hit by a truck. When he came home, he told hilarious stories about being passed by ten-year-olds on stingray bikes, eating ibuprofen like Sweet Tarts, and not being able to sit on the toilet without wincing.

As long as he was out of the house, he loved being married. He sent more postcards expressing his love for me and his thankfulness to God for bringing us together.

One postcard's front read: "I dreamed about you last night—thanks for a lovely evening." On the back, he'd written:

Hon,

Today, on the bus, God commanded that my every thought be of you. He didn't use your name but the description was clear. "Finally, whatever is true, whatever is noble, whatever is right, whatever is pure, whatever is lovely, whatever is admirable—if anything is excellent or praiseworthy—think about such things."

Phil. 4:8

I'm in love with you, Robyn,
Craig

We never knew which Craig would come home—the one who was merry and charming or the one who was ugly and controlling. For sure, when he was out of the house, he loved the *idea* of being married—the fantasyland version, where new love lasts forever and children are props and money is in endless supply.

Honestly, I liked being married to Craig better when he was out of the house. No eggshells to walk on. No fights about how long piano should be practiced or what the boys should wear to school or church. No television running all night. No porn videos carelessly left in the VCR. No pop cans, dirty dishes, and piles of paper stacked everywhere. I taped his love letters and postcards up where I could see them. Our public romance was still the envy of onlookers. I hoped that, one day, it really *would* be enviable.

In late August, Craig offered to fly Buzz, another pastor friend, to Pennsylvania. He used the delivery trip as a teaching flight. One of his student pilots, Roger, flew the left seat to satisfy a prerequisite for his pilot's license. The trip went long because of headwinds, and it was 11:00 p.m. by the time they arrived. Craig usually called me as soon as he landed to let me know he was safe, so he set off in pursuit of a pay phone since there was no cell phone service. He looked for an hour and finally gave up. At dawn's light, he called home with a full explanation and an apology before making the flight back to Grand Rapids with Roger.

He returned home with more great stories to tell—about their tricky landing and about nearly falling into a lake in the middle of the night as he walked around camp trying to find a telephone.

Seven days later, Craig flew to Pennsylvania alone to retrieve Buzz. "I won't get there till about 11:00 tonight," he said, "and I won't meet up with Buzz till tomorrow morning about 8:00. Remember the phone fiasco last time. I won't try to call tonight—I'll just call in the morning." Craig loved night flying; he always said it was the best. When I wasn't piloting, I agreed. To fly above a cushion of clouds and have the moon illuminate from above—breathtaking. Or to fly over a city full of twinkling lights—beautiful. Or to fly over a fireworks display on the Fourth of July—magical.

We talked about whether he should take the cell phone we shared, but decided that I should keep it.

In the middle of the night, I was awakened by a knock. I looked at the clock next to the bed—3:15 a.m. It could only be Craig. He must have decided not to stay overnight in Pennsylvania as planned. He could never keep track of his house key and, without one, he would have to bang on the door. I got up and looked out the bedroom window, but couldn't see his car. I checked all the doors, but there was no one there. *I must have dreamed it,* I thought as I got back into bed.

There was no call from him the next morning. As soon as I came home from dropping the boys off at school, I checked the answering machine. Nothing. Finally, the phone rang at 8:45 a.m. *What a relief,* I thought as I answered. I fully expected to hear Craig's story of peril or adventure, but it wasn't Craig. It was Buzz. "Robyn, have you heard from Craig? He isn't here yet."

"No, I haven't. But Craig is often distracted by life. Give me your cell number, and if I hear from him before he arrives, I'll let you know. Call me when he gets there." I had total confidence in Craig's ability. He had flown into airports so small that they were simply scratches carved into the geography. Many things could have prevented him from checking in. He might have had engine trouble and had to put down in a field or unscheduled airport that didn't have a phone. He might have overslept or stopped to help someone. *He's been flying for twenty-five years,* I reminded myself. *He has owned this plane for ten years. He just took this trip last week. I'm ready for him to call, Lord,* I prayed. *Make that phone ring.* I looked at my watch, again, 9:45 now. I paced.

Finally the phone rang. "Hey," Buzz asked, "do you think he got the wrong airport? Maybe he's confused about the plan."

"No, he had the airport identifier. He's always late, Buzz. He'll be there. Call me when he arrives."

At 10:45 a.m., everything in my stomach turned sour. No more rationalization. If Craig hadn't contacted me by then, it was because he couldn't—he was incapacitated.

I called our home airport for advice. "You might want to check with Flight Services," said Hank. FSS—Flight Services & Systems—told me pilots are often late to destinations and offered a variety of explanations:

weather problems, engine trouble, even fuel depletion. Since there had been no reported crashes, I was told to wait for him to turn up while they started a routine search.

FSS contacted the Federal Aviation Administration, who of course had their own questions. How long had Craig been a pilot? When did he leave? What was his disposition? Would he have diverted from the plan? Was anyone else with him? Might he have run off with anyone? Had he exhibited any unusual behavior?

"He was in good spirits. He doesn't drink or use drugs. He was alone, and I'm confident that he didn't run off," I told the FAA man.

Craig's parting remarks before any long flight were always the same: "Babelicious, if I crash, they won't need a little black box to know that my last thoughts were of you." I knew he hadn't run off with another woman.

Craig had not filed a flight plan—not uncommon for seasoned pilots taking routine flights, but it complicated the search. Without an exact departure time, flight plan, or radio communication, the search teams had to eliminate all the other flights on the radar boards across the entire flight path before they could identify Craig's flight path. Langley Air Force Base was assigned that task, using the signal from the transponder in our plane.

I prayed that the emergency locator transmitter would send out a distress signal. An ELT is supposed to keep sending its signal after a crash to help locate the plane and its occupants, but if it's underwater or buried in the ground, it's useless.

The next evening, the news shows started airing the story. The FAA and the Civil Air Patrol assured me that the search would continue as long as there were leads to follow. There wasn't much for me to do except wait.

In the midst of marital strife, it's easy for a wife to fantasize about life without a contrary husband—about being able to make decisions about money, parenting, what car to drive, or where and when to go on vacation without fighting through his objections first. It's tempting to daydream about how much better off you'd be without him. But there are things you don't contemplate—such as moving out of your house because it's too much to handle or afford, or putting the kids in daycare because you have to go to work another job. When a husband dies, you lose all the good stuff as well as the bad.

I pleaded with God for Craig's life. Despite our schizophrenic relationship, he had so much potential. He was smart and funny and charismatic. If he could just let go of the get-rich-quick schemes and find a job with a career path, if we could get some help for his anger and find our sweet spot together, if we could find our way back to the way we'd been when we dated, how wonderful that would be. How quiet and dull my life would be without him! I was besieged by memories of how he made every birthday and holiday a production, how from his plane he would buzz the house until the neighbors came out, how he would snuggle me up when I got hit by a wave of grief and hold me silently until it passed. How we would get remarried every anniversary, with a little ceremony in the pastor's office and a party following.

We'd gone to Hawaii for our first anniversary. There is a six-hour time change, and at 2:00 a.m., he woke me up insisting that I come with him to the beach. "I'm too tired!" I said, but he told me that in years to come I wouldn't remember how tired I was, but I *would* remember what he wanted to show me. Reluctantly, I followed him to a quiet beach. The sand was still warm on my feet, and the moon hung low over the ocean, just at eye level. The expanse of the ocean met the horizon of the sky well behind the enormous full white moon suspended in front of me. I ventured into the ocean for the first time in my life and was surprised at the pull of the tide. God seemed suddenly bigger and more powerful than I ever imagined. The God who had spoken that moment into existence so it would be waiting for me was surely big enough to handle all the problems I would encounter. The assurance of his love and presence, demonstrated in that moment, was burned into my memory and heart forever.

As long as I wasn't presented with a corpse, I would speak of this mission to find Craig as a rescue and not a recovery.

People hovered, wanting to help, but there was nothing for them to do. If they hung around, they would need food and beverages. I didn't want to be hospitable, I didn't want to be comforted—I wanted to curl up in a ball. I paced the house, looking out the windows like a dog waiting for the master's arrival. I expected to see him drive up or a police car deliver him like a good ending to a sappy movie.

I paused at the front window to look at his headstone grave marker in the front yard. Not everyone wants a tombstone in their yard. Craig was thrilled with his.

On a trip to Wisconsin, we'd visited his father's grave. The marker had both Willy and Almida's names on it. "Mom will be buried next to my dad," he explained.

"Isn't that weird, though?" I asked. "He's been dead for twenty years and she's been married to Bob for ten."

"Nope, that's what they want. Bob will be buried next to his first wife over there," he said, pointing across the cemetery lawn. "Together forever with the spouse of their youth."

"We should be buried together like that, with both our names on a bronze headstone."

"Really, you would do that?" His eyes welled with tears. "It's too much to ask."

"Let's do it," I said. *I'll be in heaven with Jesus, praising God,* I thought. *Will it matter where my body is?*

For Craig's next birthday, I ordered a marker with our names on it. Our wedding date was entwined in two wedding bands. "Together For-ever" was embossed below it. We hadn't bought cemetery plots, so I had it delivered and set in the front yard. Craig was beyond moved—he was speechless. He said it was the best present anyone had ever given him.

I hoped I wouldn't need it yet.

The search continued into the Great Lakes, Ohio, and Pennsylvania. The State Police, Coast Guard, and NASA joined the search. A missing person report was filed; any confused-looking, six-foot males with long, brown, curly hair and wearing a Hawaiian shirt roaming aimlessly along the flight path would be questioned.

Nothing.

A bazillion people were praying for us. My pillars, the women who had stuck with me since Jay's death and a couple who had joined me since, put their lives on hold so I would have a chance to get mine back. They spent long hours at the house with me. They phoned every airport along what we thought would be the most likely flight path, asking them to listen for Craig's ELT signal frequency. They called chambers of commerce requesting support for the search. They called radio and television stations along the flight path, asking them to run the story to increase the chances of finding Craig. They took my boys on play dates and reminded me to eat. Dave, a member of the Bible study for motorcycle enthusiasts Craig and I led at our church, put up a website to answer questions and post prayer requests and search updates.

A week into the search.

I hope for the best, but fear the worst—which I am convinced would be finding Craig alive but broken beyond restoration. Wheelchair-bound or brain-damaged becomes my new nightmare, knowing how eternally ill tempered he would be. Or—maybe the process of his recuperation, learning to live handicapped, will be the refining fire for both of us. Whatever it takes, count me in. *I love you, Lord, and I trust you to do what is best for all of us, even if it isn't what I want or what is easy.*

Everyone has been incredibly hopeful. I confess that I waver. I hope to find Craig alive and repairable, but my belly feels like I'm flying through turbulence. There's no spit in my mouth. I try to eat, but everything is texture without moisture. My clothes are getting loose, my is skin dry. My brain is telling me that it has been too long since he disappeared, and that if he were alive he would have been found by now, but my heart and the Spirit in me say that with God all things are possible. The number of days Craig has been missing doesn't matter a whit to him. Moses was on the mountain with God for forty days and nights with no food or water and came down radiant. I pray that Craig is enjoying the presence of the Lord.

A bit of good news: Langley has determined that Craig made it to Pennsylvania. The last spot his plane shows up on the radar shows that he flew into the middle of a thunderstorm near Huntingdon, Pennsylvania, and didn't come out. At first I'm excited—we know where he is! But my excitement is dampened when they tell me the radar images could narrow the search down to a 25-square-mile area in mountainous Western Pennsylvania. It's still a big haystack.

It's mostly bad news after that, when there's any news at all. Bad weather, rain, and fog keep search planes grounded and ground crews hunkered down. Over the phone, I ask Colonel Bruner, in charge of the Pennsylvania Civil Air Patrol mission, if he is giving up some intensity because he thinks they're searching for a corpse. He says in a firm, exacting voice, "If an eighty-four-year-old woman could hang from a tree for four days and survive, then Craig could certainly still be alive. We have not lost our intensity at all, ma'am. It all comes down to weather. Every resource is being brought to bear for the search." He requests additional pilots, planes, and ground forces from New York and New Jersey to join the search. All we need is some good weather.

Roger, Craig's student pilot and friend, who has been unswervingly expectant of getting Craig back alive, retraces their flight path with a pilot from our home-base airport, using a plane of his own. With five kids, he and his wife, Mary, are the busiest people I know. He's a successful businessman with huge commitments to church and missions. They bought all my plane tickets and went with me to search sites. Impatient for news, Roger and Mary hire a small plane to take us to the Civil Air Patrol command center in Pennsylvania. Getting into a small plane is a horse I have trouble remounting. I imagine the banner headline: MISSING PILOT MIRACULOUSLY FOUND, WIFE DIES IN A CRASH ON HER WAY TO THE SCENE.

We take a commercial flight instead.

We flew into Harrisburg, where we're met by a chaplain of the Civil Air Patrol. He's been assigned to me for spiritual guidance, but he doesn't believe the Bible's miracles actually happened. He tells me Jesus didn't really feed the five thousand in John 6; he merely inspired men to share their lunch. He suggests that the miracle was actually that men overcame their own selfishness. The book of Jonah, he claims, is a metaphor for inspiration. Good grief! Who would have thought the trip here would turn into a mission field for me?

At the Civil Air Patrol command post, sixty miles from the search area, Roger and I are shown a map of Craig's likely flight plan that Langley has mapped out using the process of elimination. The officers on duty ask questions about Craig's tendencies and past experiences. Then they show us the weather radar map of the area the night Craig flew into it, bearing a little yellow mark where the radar lost his signal. My heart nearly stops—there is a giant, brightly colored blob indicating the storm stretching two hundred nautical miles in front of Craig's plane dot. Storms like that create downdrafts and updrafts that cause commercial airliners to gain or lose hundreds of feet in a couple of seconds. I can only hope that he saw it on the horizon and found a place to set down. On a mountain. In the dark. Against the storm.

Civil Air Patrol pilots fly that course and also several others toward alternative airports, but find no sign of our red-and-gold plane.

I continue to pray that one Civil Air Patrol pilot will think of something that no one else has. That he will find Craig in a place that hasn't been searched before. I know it's a long shot. How do the spouses of MIA military pilots do this for years?

I feel like the Lord is pushing me to the edge. This is so hard, yet I speak with the volunteers from the Civil Air Patrol about the hope I have in God. I talk about the faith Craig and I share in Jesus, about God's miracles, about the salvation provided to his followers. I tell them, as I have so often told myself, that until I see a corpse, I will trust God for a miraculous rescue.

There are a couple of other Christians on the base, but mostly I am a curiosity. My belief that God is in control and that all things are possible baffles many here. What else can I do? If my God is enough and trustworthy for the day to day, how much more must he be enough and trustworthy for the tragic and difficult! Where else can I turn? Clearly, men are doing all they can. More sorties are being flown searching for Craig than on any other mission of record. More money and manpower will be spent trying to find him than was spent searching for John F.

Kennedy Jr. But Craig's life is in the hands of God alone. Everyone has been working so hard that I know they want nothing more than to find him. I try to remain a constant source of compliments and encouragement. They feel they have let me down, but I know no one is going to find Craig until God says yes.

On one of the flights home from Pennsylvania, I sit next to Charlie, a traveling salesman, who asks me where I am flying and why. When I tell him I'm on my way home from Pennsylvania, where the Civil Air Patrol has been looking for my missing husband, the conversation turns awkward. "How can you be so cheerful?" he asks.

"Both Craig and I love and trust Jesus," I tell him. "I have an inexplicable peace, knowing that no matter how this ordeal ends, I will be taken care of. If Craig dies, he will be in heaven with God." I ask, "Do you have any kind of spiritual grounding or faith?"

He says, "My wife is the faithful one at our house. She'll go to heaven for sure because she's so good and kind."

Gently, I say, "Being nice or good or kind are wonderful qualities, but the Bible says those traits can't get you into heaven. The Bible says there's only one way men can find eternal life with God, and that's by receiving Jesus Christ as their Savior."

I lift the plastic spork from my tray and say, "Charlie, if I bought this for you and offered it to you, you'd have to take it before it really belonged to you, right?"

He nods.

"See, it's the same with Jesus' gift of salvation. He offers it to you, it's already yours, but you have to accept it for yourself. Jesus died on a cross for the sins of man and was raised from the dead after three days in the grave, conquering death so that anyone who believes in him will have eternal life. Wouldn't you like to do that?"

Charlie declines.

I'm disappointed. I know it isn't my job to save or persuade anyone. That's God's job. But a little good news to celebrate would have been nice.

It felt good to be home. My pillars had worked tirelessly spreading the word, asking for information, keeping prayer chains updated and fresh. We sat around my table, creating silly situations about where Craig could be, imagining funny rescue scenarios, and finding some relief in laughter.

"Maybe he's still broken in the plane, and God is feeding him bugs and dew like the prophet Elijah."

"Maybe a surprised hunter or bird-watcher will call in his whereabouts."

"Maybe some widow living back in the mountains had been praying for a husband when Craig's plane crashed on her property, and now she's keeping him for herself."

"She'd have her hands full!"

Surrounded by my friends, I feel safe. The odds against having to bury two husbands in four years seem on our side. My friends have taken care of Jake and Eli while I've been gone, providing so many play dates and distractions that the boys don't want to come home, crying and carrying on when I pick them up.

God, I hate being a single parent.

At the end of the second week, I talk to the new Civil Air Patrol commander in Philipsburg, Pennsylvania. Major Don Lang's telephone briefing makes me want to stand at attention and salute. I am in good hands. The search has been reduced to a 5-square-mile area.

Mary and Roger take me back to Pennsylvania for the third time. The new base looks like something from an old movie. The command center occupies a large wooden building filled with computers on metal desks operated by people in monochromatic green jumpsuits and shiny black boots. Outside, there are tents and lots more people in the same matching color. I look like a corsage in my flowered top and sandals.

Bad weather, hazy conditions, and overcast skies frustrate the mission. Ground fog keeps the planes tied to the airfield. Ground troops swarm the mountain around the last known radar hit. The leaves have begun to take on their fall colors, and our red plane will soon be camouflaged beneath the canopy of deciduous trees. The sun peeks out for a moment at noon, only to hide again a moment later. The next day's forecast is for more of the same.

There aren't enough rooms at the motel for all of the volunteers and us too, so all in one room, Mary and I share the bed and Roger sleeps in the chair. Before returning to the base, we pray out of Psalm 121, kneeling together.

> I lift up my eyes to the mountains—
>> where does my help come from?
> My help comes from the LORD,
>> the Maker of heaven and earth.

At the camp, a cautiously excited Major Bob Meinert asks me, "Would Craig fly left seat or right seat without a passenger?"

"Probably right seat."

He seems very pleased. "In a crisis, pilots make decisions based on experience, conditions, and seating in the plane. I think Craig's emergency approach pattern might have been affected by his sitting on the right. I'm going to create an arc approach from the last radar blip based on the possibility of Craig making a right turn rather than a left on approach."

A flutter of fresh hope tickles my insides.

That change in the search parameters bears fruit. *Ground troops radio in that they have spotted the plane! Glory hallelujah! Praise God!*

"And Craig—have they found Craig?" I ask.

There is no word.

Time seems to have stopped. The atmosphere at the command post is charged. There's not a sign of weariness or discouragement as we all wait for more news. I walk outside and pray for Craig's life. *Even if he's dead, Lord—raise him!* I pray. *I'm asking for another chance at our marriage, this time with a man who has encountered God on the mountain and is forever transformed by the experience.*

An hour later, someone comes outside to find me. There is more information. People avoid my eyes. Four men in the ubiquitous green jumpsuits take me into a small room filled with bunks. Their faces tell me what they are reluctant to speak. Craig is dead.

The ground team that spotted the plane had to hike down to it to find out whether Craig was inside. The four men hesitate to give me details; they say only that Craig's body was found and assure me that he died on impact.

Although the news isn't exactly a surprise—after this amount of time, this was the most likely outcome—I am truly shocked. I have no tears; I am without words. So my first bewildered utterance is a Craigism: "This sucks." I *hate* that word. I hated when he said it, and it didn't sound any better coming out of my mouth.

Captain Randy, a Christian pilot who was one of the four men to tell me Craig was dead, whispers an admonishment to me as we walk back toward the command center. "People will be watching your reaction to the news," he says. "You've been such a strong testimony to them up to this point . . ." He smiles sympathetically.

It's just what I need to hear. I collect myself. It's important—to the search crew and to me—that I testify that God is enough even when the news is bad. Because he is.

The wreckage was found five miles northwest of Mount Union in the heavily forested mountains of Western Pennsylvania, about 135 miles east of Pittsburgh. The Civil Air Patrol assigned a driver to me. It took two hours to drive to the area. Since they came from a different camp, Roger and Mary met me near the hiking trail we would take to the plane. CAP volunteers guided Roger, Mary, and me on a ninety-minute hike to a spot from which we could see the crash site.

It's no wonder the plane hadn't been seen from the air. From our vantage point on a ridge, the plane wreckage could barely be seen five hundred yards below us. A canopy of leaves camouflaged it from above. It must have been tossed like a dart through the trees, not even breaking off the limbs as it passed in the strong winds from the storm. Above, a Civil

Air Patrol search airplane circled, unable to spot the wreckage even while using the longitudinal and latitudinal coordinates from the ground team.

We hiked partway down the mountain to get a closer look. The plane was buckled at the cockpit with the tail flipped back over itself like a distressed yoga position. One wing was two lengths behind the fuselage. Although I was too far away to see Craig's body, it was reported to me that he was seat belted inside the cockpit, his legs still inside the fuselage, but his torso not. The remains were unidentifiable after all those nights of exposure to elements and the animals.

I know if it had been me who crashed, Craig would have gone to my broken, rotting corpse. He would have wanted that story to tell. He would have said he loved me too much not to say a final good-bye. He would have said I was still beautiful to him.

I didn't have the courage. I didn't want that to be my last image of Craig.

In the airport terminal, waiting for our flight home, Roger and Mary assured me that they would walk with me through the grieving process. I had no doubt. I have great friends.

The night sky outside the airliner window was a comforting blanket. I said good-bye to my husband. I would never look at another full moon without thinking of how many he had shown me from vantage points around the world.

It was late when we landed in Grand Rapids. I drove home alone to an empty house. My request. I wanted a few hours before I had to face it all.

I wandered through the quiet house, lingering in the dining room. The postcards and letters Craig had sent me from recent adventures were still hanging from the plate shelf. The last one read:

Robyn,

Every day I wake up I know how fortunate I am. The overwhelming love I feel from you is so very humbling. I have never done anything in my life, not even for one moment, to deserve the likes of you. You are the most precious, most marvelous, most endearing woman to have ever walked the face of this earth. I will never be able to fathom how I ever got myself into the position for you to pick me, but I will always marvel at the fact that I did. The direct result has been a most enchanting experience. My life has become more joyous and full than I could have dreamed. Real life has eclipsed every fantasy.

I'm in love with you, Robyn. And I don't say that lightly. I'll back it with the last drop of my blood. I'll back it with the last breath that I take. I'll back it with the last beat of my heart. The life that I have only exists because you are in it. You mean everything to me.

I love you, Robyn,
Craig

XOXOXOXOXOXO

I would miss the man who wrote those love letters.

Chapter 14

STARTING OVER— AGAIN

I knew what was coming and I didn't want to face it.

The pain.

The fear.

The loneliness.

The questions.

There was no avoiding it. The phone started ringing early the next morning and was relentless for days. I felt small and fragile with no mama and no husband. I didn't want to talk on the phone, repeating painful details. I didn't want to speculate about what had happened to cause the crash or what thoughts might have crossed Craig's mind in the moments before impact. I didn't want to graciously listen to other women tell me their dead husband stories or that time was my friend. I didn't want strangers' unsolicited advice for getting through this; I didn't want to try to come up with an answer when asked how much tragedy one family can bear. I wasn't ready to be encouraging to those who, like me, were devastated by Craig's death.

I didn't want to—and yet I did all those things.

People tried to console me by saying, "At least he died doing what he loved." I nodded and smiled, but churned inside. Craig used to say, "If I die in the airplane, don't let anyone say I died doing what I loved to do. Tell them I loved *you*. Tell them I did something stupid and it killed me." Craig could say things like that. I couldn't—even if I had wanted to. I kept just how careless he had been to myself. He hadn't checked the weather before the flight. He chose to maintain his course even when he saw the flashes of lightning on the horizon. He decided to take the risk, and it killed him. It killed our marriage. It killed our future.

I functioned on autopilot. Take care of the kids. Call the pastor. Plan the funeral. Find places for out-of-town visitors to stay. Make travel arrangements for the trip to Wisconsin for the Treu family memorial service. Get my hair colored.

The lovely Victorian funeral parlor we used for Jay and his folks was nearly impossible to get to because of road construction. I'd have to find another place. I began shopping for a funeral parlor. I wanted it to be warm and inviting, spacious, and preferably pink. It's ridiculous the things you place importance on, but in my mind, I was sure it would help me to stand in a pink room in a pink dress. Some places were dark—not the tone I wanted to set. Some were too sterile or too contemporary. Several were pale green, which I rejected immediately because green is simply not a flattering shade for my skin tone—especially without makeup. As I walked briskly through lobbies and labyrinths, funeral associates—who tend to be gentle and kind by disposition and professional training—would hurry along with me. "Are you preplanning a funeral for yourself or someone else?" they would ask.

"No, I'm not preplanning. It's for my husband."

"Is he ill?"

"No … he's already dead," I answered as I walked.

"Oh, I am so sorry. May I ask what happened?"

"Well, he crashed our airplane into the side of a mountain. He's in Pennsylvania now, being autopsied. His body will be shipped to me and I'll need someone to take over here in town."

"I saw that story on the news! So he's been located?"

"Yes, yesterday. I came from Pennsylvania last night."

"I'm glad he was found. I'm sorry it had to end that way."

"Me too. Do you have a room decorated in any shade of pink? I kind of have my heart set on a pink room."

"Let me show you what we offer. Would you like to look at caskets too?"

"I'm not sure—I think he'll already be in one, won't he? He's been dead awhile—I don't think they'd ship his body in a cardboard box or a body bag."

"He is probably in a casket. We can choose an ornamented one from our selection. I can certainly help you with all the transportation arrangements. Do you know where his final resting place will be or do you need assistance selecting a plot?"

"Hmm. Well, I suppose I should bury him in the cemetery across the street from the house. That's where my other husband is buried. It would make it easier for me to visit."

Pause.

"I see."

Pause again.

"What about a headstone?"

"Oh, I already have that. It's in the front yard of my house. It will have to be moved. Can you arrange that?"

"Of course." Never missed a beat. Those guys have heard it all.

The ninth funeral home I visited was just about perfect. Close to home, good parking—and a large room draped in pink window treatments, pink patterned carpet, and a pretty pink, mauve, and gray wall covering. Excellent! "I'll take it."

Craig's body was flown to Grand Rapids in a metal, military-looking casket. I arranged a private visitation for the family to say good-bye. There was no body to view; the casket arrived from Pennsylvania closed and sealed. I had time to sit with it before Craig's family arrived. I wept. I sobbed. I grieved the lost future. Alone, I banged on the casket in anger. Angry that he'd been so stupid and so selfish. Angry about his unrealized potential as a husband, as a father, and as the man God created him to be. I slumped onto the floor next to the metal box. He got off so easy!

I was the one left to clean up his mess. Again. This was not happily-ever-after. This was not what I'd signed up for.

By the time Craig's family arrived, I was composed. When his mom, Almida, saw the metal box, she draped herself over it, sobbing deeply. Others tried to comfort her. Her husband rubbed her back and her other son, Bruce, kept saying, "It's okay, Mom. It's okay." I just watched. There was nothing for me to say. Her agony was profound, so intimate, it was hard to watch. I knew there was no comfort for the pain she felt. It was *not* okay, and it would be a long time before *okay* came close to describing her.

Days were filled with relatives and visitors, in person and on the phone. Food, comforting words, and offers to pray for us flooded in. The letter carrier had to deliver mail to the front door because the volume of cards wouldn't fit in the mailbox. It was balm for my broken heart to be encouraged by so many.

Pastor Ed Dobson officiated at Craig's funeral in the same chapel where Jay's funeral service had been four years before and where Craig and I had been married two and a half years earlier. The room was full. There were lots of tears shed, lots of cake eaten, and lots of hysterically funny Craig stories exchanged. Everyone had something good to say about the dead guy.

Craig was buried in Michigan, in the same cemetery as Jay. The year before, Craig had been furious with Jake because he had dinged one of the tiny roses on the corner of the bronze tombstone in our front yard with the lawn mower. Jake was only ten at the time, and it had been an accident, but Craig had carried on like Rumpelstiltskin, saying that the marker was ruined and that he would *never* be buried under it.

Turns out, he would be.

The jury was out on whether I would be too. I was only forty-four, and I was hoping for many more years before a decision about my final resting place would need to be made.

The following week, Stuart Briscoe led a memorial service for the Treu side of the family at Elmbrook Church in Milwaukee. I didn't know most of the hundreds of people at that service. It was predominantly attended by friends and relatives of Craig's family whom I'd never met. I know the reunion helped his mom. She saw people who only show up for significant life events like funerals.

Through it all, God granted me his peace. He infused me with strength to be a voice of comfort to others. His character overshadowed mine. I was able to be the gracious, grieving widow others needed me to be. I was kind to people who bordered on obnoxious with their questions. I was gentle and encouraging with those whose faith was shaken because they had been so sure Craig would be found and rescued. I listened attentively to advice about grieving as if I had no experience with it.

The day Craig's personal effects arrived, another wave of loss washed over me. His wallet smelled like sweet grass clippings, and the aeronautical watch I'd given him for our anniversary was still running. Until I held his wedding ring in my hand, I think I was still waiting to hear that it had all been some kind of mistaken identity mix-up. But there it was, the irrefutable evidence. Someone had polished the ring; it looked like no one had ever worn it. As if all our history had been buffed away with the dead flesh.

We, that is to say I, re-implemented the rule of thankfulness. As we had after Jay died, the children and I shared daily how God had met a need or how someone had intersected our day in a positive way.

There was plenty to be thankful for. I was thankful for all the people who had helped me during the search for Craig and with my reorientation to my new life.

I was thankful for all I'd learned. I could read a map, navigate Chicago traffic, and fly an airplane. I rode motorcycles with confidence. I had seen the Atlantic and Pacific oceans. I had learned to ballroom dance, snow ski, and host a dinner party for thirty people using stemware and cloth napkins.

I was exceedingly thankful that Craig had been found—on the very last day of the search. *The very last day!* I had closure. I was able to move forward. One of the curses of having a missing spouse is that you need to carry on as if you're married, even though it doesn't look or feel as if you are. If his body had not been found, I would have been compelled to keep the same routines with the children as if he were alive and coming back. Any changes to the house would have been limited to maintenance. Decisions about what to do with the stocks he was gambling/day-trading would have been filtered through the possibility that I would have to defend those decisions to Craig should he return.

I confess I was especially thankful that Craig was done parenting my children. All my anxiety about that dissolved on the side of the mountain. I was exceedingly thankful for that.

⚜

Within a month I realized the fears I'd experienced after Jay died about being a widowed single parent felt more like freedom after Craig died. Freedom to go, do, say, wear, buy, drive, and parent without considering a husband's opinion. Submission was no longer a gift I was expected to offer, much less a requirement I had to satisfy.

Because I was emotionally ill equipped to tackle a move, we stayed on in our Easter-egg-yellow farmhouse. I pitched out Craig's girly magazines and porn videos. I put the television from our bedroom at the curb with a big *FREE* sign on it. I couldn't imagine moving or even sorting the storage area full of Craig's personal treasures and collectables: Franklin Mint plates, Betty Boop and Lenox figurines, myriad chess sets, trinkets and souvenirs from his adventures filled shelves from floor to ceiling. I just shut the door on it all. Then there was still Jay's garage full of toolboxes, giant compressors, and welding equipment to consider. No, we would stay put and I would deal with the accumulation later.

I was deliberate in preserving the best of my dead husband. I was careful not to dishonor or idolize him. He was gone, and we would have to forge a new life without him. Like Jay, Craig was relegated to photographs that captured happy times and to the stories we shared about him. Just as Jay's drug and alcohol use became a thing of the distant past, memories of Craig's crushing words and punitive sanctions gave way to smiles and laughter. Every good day multiplied the distance since the last bad one.

I went back to teaching Bible study at church. The timing was perfect. It seemed as if every time I had a fearful thought, it would be addressed in the study material that week. I had been assigned a small group of new believers and seekers to lead. I lavished the currency of my recent experiences on them, exchanging my understanding of God's love and sovereignty for their many questions.

Worry about money abated. People sent cards filled with words of encouragement and money. Hundreds of dollars in checks, cash, and gift cards to McDonald's piled up. The airplane had been insured for the tidy sum of $32,000. The inheritance checks from my mom's estate had stopped, but my survivor benefits from Social Security were reinstated until Eli turned sixteen, which gave me about seven years to find a way to replace that income. Our living expenses were manageable even on our fixed income since I no longer had to bear the costs of Craig's cavorting or the monthly overhead for airport fees, aircraft maintenance, and aviation fuel. After I liquidated the stocks Craig had been "trading," I had a little nest egg back in the bank.

I stayed on at the dental office. The additional income helped, as did getting out and focusing on something other than being a widow—again. The boys stayed at their school, with teachers who were familiar with their circumstances and willing to guide them gently through their grieving process.

My pillars filled in the gaps for the next year. They decorated my house with flamingo lights and goofy signs for my birthday. We got dressed up and went out to fancy restaurants for "date nights." They carved pumpkins with us for Halloween, invited us to join their families for the holidays, and sent me Valentine's chocolates in February.

Just as when Jay died, God blanketed me with his grace and peace. I was encouraged and supported by his Body. I found my strength in God and his people and they carried me as I grieved and as I healed.

It took a while, but I made it.

Chapter 15

ALMOST HAPPILY EVER AFTER

W ell, one thing was for sure. I. Was. Done. Being. Married. Good grief! Can you blame me? You need a reason? I had lots of reasons.

I didn't think any husband could love me as much as the one before.

I didn't want my kids to have to adjust to another dad—or lose another dad.

I thought God would leave me single so he would get all the credit for our survival, our ability to function, our healing. After I married Craig, so many people said, "Oh, good, you're married again. That makes everything better." But, as *anyone* who has been married for more than fifteen minutes will tell you, just being married does not always make everything better.

And, honestly, the line of men to date a woman with kids who has buried two husbands in four years is *very* short!

But God had other plans. I'd like to think it's because I'm such good wife material and he didn't want all that talent to go to waste, but it's just as likely that he knows I need constant supervision!

Enter Dave, Mr. 4-Ever.

Dave was part of the biker Bible study Craig and I led. He'd shown up about eighteen months before Craig died, all excited about his faith, as new believers often are. "I just discovered that Jesus Christ is God

Almighty! Why didn't anyone ever tell me that before?" he exclaimed when he first introduced himself.

Back then, he was like a lost puppy, so quiet and soft-spoken that I had him pegged as timid at best, pitiful at worst. Tall and lean, with nearly black, wavy hair and pure blue eyes, he wore plaid shirts and double-knee work pants over the long underwear that peeked out at his neckline and socks. He'd grown up on a lake—not one of those swanky lakes with big houses and speedboats, but the kind rimmed with little cottages and scruffy men who fish off bass boats that sparkle like a kindergartner's glitter art project. The kind with a trailer park you can see from the shore. Dave liked to hunt and fish and cold-weather camp in tents. Blech! He had graduated from high school with a fifth-grade reading level and had to go to thirteenth grade at the junior college to improve his reading skill.

Dave joined our study shortly after the girl he'd been shacking up with cheated on him—then dumped him. Like a toppling line of dominos, he lost the girl, the house, custody of their family pet, and his business.

In an effort to get his life back on track, he started reading the Bible and listening to Christian radio. God spoke to him through the pages and through the preachers on the Calvary Satellite Network radio station. As if Dave was his only listener, the guy on the radio said, "You want to know truth? Then you got to get yourself to a church where they teach the Bible from cover to cover." So Dave started attending our church. A short time later, as part of a series on community, the guy on the radio said, "You need more than Sunday services in this life, son. You need to get into a small group with other believers." That's how he found himself in our group of motorcycle enthusiasts. He was full of questions. Not about who God was or whether he was real—he had settled that part. Dave wanted to know how to engage with what the Holy Spirit was doing on earth every day.

I felt kind of sorry for him. He was a really nice guy, but he was so banged up. I started praying for a wife for him—he *needed* one! At thirty-five, Dave had never been married or had children. He wanted a wife who would stay at home, have a couple of kids, maybe bake him an apple pie once in awhile. He wasn't a chauvinist; he was a traditionalist.

Dave thought I was ugly-bossy and way too talkative. So he started praying for *Craig*! He told me later he couldn't figure out how anyone could stand being married to me. (You just wait, mister.)

By the time Craig died, Dave's life had shifted. His heart had mended. He was gainfully employed as a maintenance supervisor at an apartment complex. And his opinion of me had shifted too. Watching me go through the search and the aftermath, watching me trust in God, Dave stopped thinking of me as a Chatty Cathy bossy-pants and started to see me as a woman of authentic faith.

In the months following Craig's death, I mentioned some of the issues I was having with my house. The water heater was demon possessed; it only worked intermittently. There was a hole in the ceiling from an old leak. The fan in the bathroom sounded like a jet engine. The driveway was cracking, and so on and so on. God spoke to Dave again: It seemed like every passage Dave read in the Bible was about taking care of widows and orphans. So he offered me his services.

Dave came from a long line of builders and inventors and could fix just about anything. He drove a big ugly van full of tools and he always had a red handkerchief in his back pocket, handy for wiping noses and smudges. I was happy for the help and put a list of man jobs on the refrigerator. Dave would drop by the house after finishing his maintenance job to tackle them for me.

I worked at the dental office till 7:30 some evenings, so Dave would hang out with the boys till I got home. He was great with them. He jumped on the trampoline with Eli or squirted him with the water hose till Eli surrendered in a fit of giggles. He took Jake to testosterone hangouts like pawn shops and gun-and-knife shows. He admired Jake's motorcycle drawings and Eli's Lego sculptures. He listened to their chatter and asked about their dreams.

I knew it was important that they have a man in their lives, and Dave seemed like an excellent choice. He didn't lie, bluster, or brag. He always did what he said he would do. Sundays, he would often sit with us at church. One week a bombshell of a woman in a tight orange dress crossed the room in front of us. I couldn't take my eyes off her. I turned to Dave, "Criminy! You don't see that kind of perfection every day, do you?"

He looked up from the floor. "I don't look," he said. "When I see something or someone I think will stick in my memory for the wrong reason, I bounce my eyes to something else."

I was dumbfounded. Who was this guy?

Not only did Dave have great character and fix everything we broke or plugged up, he was a true wilderness man. He hunted with a bow and arrows. He owned a slew of firearms. He knew how to start a fire without matches. He could horse trade at the gun-and-knife shows. He made yard work and cleaning the garage fun! My boys were in heaven.

Even though he had nothing to gain by it, he took care of me, the kids, the house, the yard, and the cars. He was drawn to the Jesus in me, to my faith, and was willing to trade menial tasks around the house for the opportunity to talk about God. None of his friends had any kind of relationship with Jesus, and he was hungry for more than a once-a-week Bible study discussion.

Sometimes he came over when I wasn't working late. A pleasant routine developed. He'd fix my leaky faucets, kill my computer viruses, or move heavy boxes around, and I'd feed him much-appreciated home-cooked meals. After supper, we'd play with the boys till bedtime, then we'd watch a show on television or talk about Jesus.

We spent some very comfortable time together, but there were no sparks. I was not the package he was looking for, and I wasn't looking for a package at all.

Remember, I was done being married.

I was way past the stage of life he wanted to initiate.

Most Sundays, a bunch of us went out for lunch together after church. One week, our crowd was packed around a big table at a Mexican restaurant, and when our meals were served one of the other men looked at Dave and said, "Why don't you pray for us?"

I froze. I knew Dave wasn't accustomed to praying out loud and certainly not in public and not in front of all these folks.

We bowed our heads and a lovely prayer of grace spilled out of his mouth.

When he looked up at me, I winked at him. "Great job, Big Shooter."

That, he told me later, is when his blinders fell off. The thought, *Hey, she's a hottie!* was followed immediately by *Uh oh, that's bad! She doesn't want what I want!*

He kept those feelings to himself for quite a while, but there were subtle hints. Some couples from church had signed up to take ballroom dancing lessons. I missed dancing, so Dave and I signed up too. (Me exuberantly, Dave reluctantly.) One evening he showed up for dance class/widow-duty showered and wearing clean clothes. Rather than work boots, sexy cowboy boots shone below his well-fitted jeans.

Smiling broadly, he said, "Hi, ready to go dancing?"

I caught a whiff of his cologne. I smacked his shoulder with the palm of my hand and said, "You are not on a date. I do not date. We do not date!"

"I know!" he said indignantly. "I just thought it would be nice to get cleaned up before I came over for a change. Don't worry, it won't happen again."

"Fine. I just don't want any mixed signals. Don't wreck things, okay?"

The truth is, I valued his handy work and his companionship. I loved his influence on my boys. We operated like an amicably divorced couple, and that suited me just fine. I had all the advantages and no commitment.

It wasn't enough for Dave. A short time later, he came over, and I knew something was up.

"We have to talk," he said, standing in the doorway. "The feelings I have for you have changed, grown stronger. I know you said you don't want to get married again, but I need to tell you how I feel. If you don't feel the same way, then I can't spend so much time here. I can still be around to help some with the boys, but I can't spend time with you."

Ugh! Really? This is going to screw everything up.

"Sorry, Dave. I got nothing here. I don't want to lead you on. I like things the way they are."

"I figured as much. I just wanted to clear the air." He turned and walked away, but he didn't stay away.

Just speaking his feelings out loud lightened something. He didn't spend as much time with me, but he was still around for the boys, still took care of the house as if he owned it. Pretty soon our relationship was right back to the way it was before "the talk."

We had a ball together. For me, it was the best of both worlds. I had a man in my life willing to keep my house in order, spend quality time with the boys, and go home at night.

It was too good to last. Dave wanted more. Finally he said, "My feelings for you haven't gone away. I can't be here anymore. I can't spend time with you knowing that you don't feel the way I do. I can't keep investing in the boys, knowing that I will never be more than Mr. Dave. It's too painful. I'm sorry, but I need to move on."

"I don't know what to say. I value you and our friendship, and I really like our time together, but I don't have any romantic feelings for you."

"So that's it then."

"That's it."

After he left, I fell apart. He had opened his umbrella of protection over me, the boys, the vehicles, and the property. Suddenly, he had closed that umbrella and taken it with him. I couldn't blame him, but it sunk me.

Dave called the next day to see how I was. He was downright gleeful to hear my snuffling.

We met for lunch to try to sort out the mess. "So what do we do now?" asked Dave, expecting that my misery stemmed from a change of heart.

"I don't know! I don't want you to go away, but I honestly don't have any romantic interest in you. I don't even think I want to get married again. I don't want to make room in my heart or my house. And I don't know that, if I did want to get married, you would be the guy. I'm a really strong woman, Dave, and I will run over you. That will make us both miserable."

It wasn't exactly what he wanted to hear, but he wasn't ready to let me go either.

"Tell you what," said Dave, "let's just take things one day at a time."

"What does *that* mean?"

"Well, you know how I feel, and judging by the mess you are today, I think there must be a little something about me that you like. Let's just take it slow. Keep an open mind, no pressure, and let's just see if anything develops."

"You'll go forward without any promises that things will change?"

"Yup. I'm leaving for Bike Week in Daytona, Florida, in a couple of days, and we'll talk again when I get back. All right?"

I was relieved that he was opening that umbrella again, but uneasy about what it all meant and how it would work out.

I didn't know what to do. While he drove to Florida for Bike Week, merrily singing to himself, "I'm going to marry that girl," I paced the floor, fretting. I really cared about Dave. He was a great guy. He loved Jesus. But he was a redneck carpenter who wanted to make babies!

The truth is, I *had* planned on marrying again—but not till after the boys were out of the house. And I had already decided the kind of man I would marry: Someone wealthy and accomplished. Someone educated and cultured. Someone brave and heroic. Someone like a Bruce Wayne (Batman's secret identity), but who followed Jesus.

Someone impossible to find.

That way, I wouldn't have to surrender my independence. Or let anyone parent my kids except me.

My commitment to go slow with Dave was still a commitment to go … somewhere. Presumably to the altar. And I was pretty sure Dave didn't want to wait until Eli left for college.

I journaled. I prayed. I listed the pros and cons.

He was terrific with the boys. Would it be wrong to marry him so they could have a man like Dave for a dad?

Maybe he'd grow on me.

But maybe not.

Ugh.

I called my friend Jennifer for counsel. "I just don't know. He deserves a woman who's wild about him. He wants children. He wants to *make* children. I'm forty-four! I am done having kids. And he's so mild-mannered. And rural. And skinny."

"Robyn, you make it sound like he can't conjugate a verb or speak in full sentences!" said Jennifer. "If you can't see all his great qualities, his strength, and that he loves you and the boys, and that he is a man of excellent character, well, then, you're just stupid!"

I was speechless.

Then the blinders fell off *my* eyes. "Oh my God, you're right!"

I looked at Dave with fresh eyes.

I had been judging his acceptability as a husband on external markers and ancient history and using those things as excuses not to consider his proposal seriously.

Yes, he had graduated with a fifth-grade reading level, but he'd gone to college to learn what he'd missed in high school. He'd done so well in his studies that he'd gone on to learn not only English but Spanish as well. He liked the study of Spanish so much that he'd spent nearly a year of his university experience in Spain. And while living in Spain, he'd traveled all over Europe, creating a documentary of the experience. He had won multiple awards for his films and video productions.

Educated and accomplished—check.

Yes, he worked as a maintenance man, but it wasn't his only gig. He also owned a film and video production business, catering to corporate clients and politicians. He kept an office downtown and could secure tickets to sold-out shows, find the best parking, and navigate the traffic like a pro.

Urban savvy and confident—check.

Yes, he was a wilderness man. He owned a vast collection of camping gear and tents. But he also owned Armani suits and a tailored tuxedo. He opened all my doors, stood when I entered a room, and handled himself with the diplomacy of a statesman. He could survive in the harshest environs outdoors, but he also thrived in the cutthroat corporate world.

Cultured and brave—check.

The only thing he didn't have was a fat bank account.

So there it was. Was I so shallow or insecure that I'd let money stand as the only reason not to consider him?

No excuses left.

I prayed, "God, don't let me make a mistake. Is Dave going to be a good man for me and for the children?"

What I heard God say was, "Look at his character."

He was patient.

He was steady.

He was a hard worker.

He was honest.

He was great with his mom and my kids.

He was an attentive listener.

He was kind.

He was generous.

I also noticed what I'd paid no attention to before: he was really quite handsome.

When Dave got back from Florida, the first words out of my mouth were, "I'm ready to get married. Let's set the date!"

That's when I learned that Dave was definitely strong enough to stand up to pressure—even to me.

"Whoa, whoa, whoa. What happened here? I thought we agreed to take it one day at a time?"

"No, *you* thought I needed time to get used to the idea of marrying you. I'm used to it. So now I'm ready to set the date."

"Well, you may be ready, but there are other people who aren't."

"What are you talking about?" I knew darn well that Dave hadn't changed his mind. Both children adored him and my mom was dead. Who else was there to consider?

"Well, for one thing, we need to give Jake and Eli time to adjust. I've always been Mr. Dave, the buddy, and now we'll be moving to something deeper. I want them to know that I *chose* them and give them some time to choose me back as their dad. I want to be their father, not just the guy you're married to now."

Oh, that is so sweet. "I can see that."

"You'll need to let your dead husbands' families know, and I think you should ask them if they have any reservations about us."

"*All* of them?" I was a trifle bitter about the way some of my ex-in-laws had distanced themselves from us. "Are you out of your cotton-pickin' mind? Why would I want to solicit their opinions?"

"Because it's the right thing to do. If I were them, I would want to know that the guy who was going to help shape Jake and Eli's future was sincere."

"I don't think it's necessary."

"I do," he said in that way that is so sincere it makes you want to cooperate. "I'd like everyone involved in Jake and Eli's life to be included so there aren't any hurt feelings or *I told you so's*. I know I'm the right man to be their dad, and I want their other dads' families to know me too." He was gentle with his words, but they were statements, not options.

Harrumph. "Okay, that makes sense," I said, capitulating, but wondering which dead husband's relatives would rub their hands with glee when given the opportunity to offer an opinion.

"And I'd like you to ask your dad to give us his blessing."

"My dad? Dave, I am forty-five years old. I'm sure he'll approve."

"It's important, Robyn. I'm going to ask my dad too. Even though he hasn't been a great role model for me, it seems like every time I open my Bible, I see something about honoring fathers and mothers. I think this is a good way to honor them, by asking them to be part of our courtship."

"If you say so. I guess that'll be nice." I was so glad my mom wasn't alive to squawk about me asking my dad for his blessing. Whew.

Then it hit me: "Wait. Did you say courtship?"

"Yeah. For years I looked for the right woman. Then God told me to be the right man so when I found her I'd be ready. I believe I am ready now, and I've been reading about courtship as an alternative to dating."

"What's the difference?"

"Well, in a courtship, the intention is that you are working toward marriage, not just sex, or filling time on a schedule."

"Oh, okay."

"I want to be a model for Jake and Eli and preserve your reputation in the neighborhood and in general. I'll still be leaving by 10:00 at night, maybe a little later on weekends. I don't want my car in your driveway later than that, encouraging gossip. I think we should still spend most of our time together in groups of people, like we've been doing on Sundays and going to dancing classes. When it's just us or the four of us, we'll spend most of our time outside or in public places."

There was a moment of hesitation before he added, "Oh, and I decided a long time ago: I'm not kissing another woman until she's my wife."

"What did you say?"

"I said, no kissing until we're married."

"Is kissing code for something else, or do you really mean no kissing? Like with our lips?"

"I really mean no kissing. When you start kissing, that's all you want to do. And once that engine gets going, it's hard to shut 'er down."

He almost lost me there, but I decided to let it ride. I would test him later.

And I did. And as hard as I tried, I couldn't get him to cave.

Finally, I wheedled a good-night kiss from him, and it was a dandy. After about seven seconds, he gently pulled away.

"Don't go," I whispered.

"I have to," he said softly. "I don't want to stop. I'm sorry, I shouldn't have let that happen."

It didn't happen again. He kept us so pure. He never so much as put his hand on my backside until we were properly and legally wed. I earned the right to wear my white wedding dress. But all that waiting made me very reluctant to take it off.

We were so eager to get married that we scheduled the ceremony at 10:30 in the morning, with an afternoon reception. Yup, same chapel and same pastor for Jay's funeral, my wedding to Craig, and Craig's funeral. Pastor Ed began with, "Well, we're here to marry Robyn … again." Dave's family smiled politely. Mine burst out laughing.

I don't know what I was thinking having the wedding so early in the day. When we arrived at the hotel for the first night of our honeymoon, it was still broad daylight outside. I was *not* going to take my dress off in that lighting.

Seeing my hesitation, Dave sat patiently as I explained the effects of gravity and nursing babies on a woman's body. I kept babbling about how women at forty-five who have had babies look a lot different than women who are fit and firm at twenty or thirty. (*Dang, why didn't I start exercising!*)

It's one thing to get naked with a man who has helped contribute to the deterioration of your body. It's quite another to reveal that same body to a man who has never seen the ravaging effects of labor, delivery, and nursing.

But finally I screwed up the courage to let the dress drop to the floor as the sunlight streamed through the window, revealing all my flaws. And all I remember Dave saying is, "Wow! You were worth the wait."

It was all good after that.

∽

Dave moved to our Easter-egg-yellow house on a busy street in town. I know. It seemed odd to me too. Three husbands, one address. But Dave didn't want the boys to be disrupted with a move. They were stable and secure in the house they had always lived in. He did, however, insist on a new bed for our bedroom.

I can honestly say he's my favorite husband. I call him Mr. 4-Ever—because he's my fourth husband and it feels like we've been together forever. Not the *ugh*, eye-rolling, sarcastic f o r e v e r, but the fits-like-an-old-shoe, comfortable forever.

And I'm the best wife he's ever had!

The boys started calling Dave Dad on our wedding day. He adopted them the following year.

Is it happily ever after?

No, it's more like beauty for ashes.

EPILOGUE

Dave and I have forged a great team at home and in ministry. Our strengths and weaknesses dovetail instead of clash (almost all the time). Jake and Eli are all grown up now, but they walked into manhood with all the skills they needed to win at life. They know they are loved to the moon and back by their mom, their dad, and their Savior. They know how to solve problems, work hard, and ask for help. They speak well of others, go out of their way to help strangers, would never hit a girl, use firearms safely, and bounce their eyes off bombshells and bimbos. They can parallel park big vehicles and back up a truck with a trailer attached to it. They both spin a good yarn and laugh heartily at the slightest excuse.

My heart's desire now that the kids are launched is to be a beacon of hope to other women. To speak strength and healing into them for a better life, using my story and God's Word to encourage, equip, and energize their faith in God.

When I find women who have made a big mess and think it's too late for them, I want to grab them and tell them it's not! I found Jesus so late. But not *too* late. It's never too late.

I want to remind women who have done everything right and yet their world falls apart anyway, that while circumstances may be out of our control they are never out of God's, and he is faithful.

I want to soothe the pain of women who have found themselves in a place of desolation or danger. I want to tell them about a God who loves them and didn't design them to be used or abused.

There is still so much about God that I don't understand. But I have learned to trust him. I want everyone to have what I have, know the Jesus

I know, and believe Who I believe. I am eager to share my story and my wisdom for getting here.

Everyone has a story. You just read mine.

God was enough for me.

And he was faithful to me. Sometimes he waited until the eleventh hour, but he was always faithful.

He will be all that and more for you too.

Isaiah 61:1–3

The Spirit of the Sovereign Lord is on me,
    because the Lord has anointed me
    to proclaim good news to the poor.
He has sent me to bind up the brokenhearted,
    to proclaim freedom for the captives
    and release from darkness for the prisoners,
to proclaim the year of the Lord's favor
    and the day of vengeance of our God,
to comfort all who mourn,
    and provide for those who grieve in Zion—
to bestow on them a crown of beauty
    instead of ashes,
the oil of joy
    instead of mourning,
and a garment of praise
    instead of a spirit of despair.
They will be called oaks of righteousness,
    a planting of the Lord
    for the display of his splendor.

Robyn, Glenda, and Dion, 1977

Craig and Jay, 1979

Robyn and Jay's wedding dance, June 1982

Jay, Andy (Grandpa with the big belly), Granny Helen holding
Jake, Robyn, and Ziggy the devil dog, December 1988

Jay working from home, with Jake and Eli assisting, 1993

Andy and Jake, 1994

Eli with
Grandma G,
1994

Jake, Jay Eli, Robyn, and Andy
Easter time, 1995

Robyn and Glenda, Easter time, 1995

Jay's Green Bay Packer-draped casket, October, 1996

Jake, Robyn, and Eli, Winter 1997

Eli and Jake, 1997

Robyn, Craig, Eli, and Jake
Wedding day, January 1998

Robyn's dad, "Tub," and his
wife Sandy, January, 1998

Robyn and Craig date night, 1999

Adoption Day,
December, 1999

Robyn at the crash site, September, 2000

Robyn with Craig's mom, Almida at the grave site
after the funeral September, 2000

Robyn at the gravesite September, 2000

Robyn celebrating her birthday with her pillars;
standing, left to right: Kari, Elaine, Robyn, Mary;
seated: Denise and Jennifer, 2000

Eli, Robyn, and Jake 2001

Dave and Robyn,
Motorcycle skills contest,
Summer 2001

Robyn, Jake, Dave,
and Eli, Wedding Day,
October 2001

Eli, Dave, Robyn, Jake,
Adoption Day,
September 2003

Eli, Dave, Robyn,
and Jake 2014

Discover even MORE
with Robyn Dykstra!

Robyn's heart is for you to continually draw closer to God. Find a wealth of life-changing resources:

- **Allow Your Marriage to Transform Your Home**
- **Learn Practical Parenting Solutions**
- **Find Joy in Your Challenges**
- **Begin to Pray Expectantly**
- **Discover the Worthiness God Sees in You**
- **Leave a Legacy of Grace and Godliness**

Get a **FREE** video from Robyn when you join her email list!

robyndykstra.com/join

If you enjoyed her story,
Wait until you see her LIVE!

Invite
Robyn!

Discover why people
are saying:
"Robyn Dykstra is the BEST
speaker I've seen!"

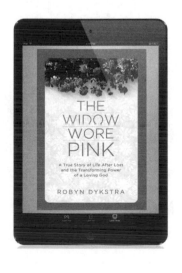

You Were Made for Matrimony

In this hour-long teaching Robyn shares lessons she's learned on her marriage journey with stories of wisdom, humor, and authenticity.

If God created marriage and pronounced it good, why is it such hard work? "Made for Matrimony" will show you the tremendous influence you carry to change your marriage and ultimately shift the atmosphere of your home.

You will laugh at familiar scenes from your own relationship as Robyn recounts personal stories that led her to a new place of belonging, appreciation, and acceptance with her husband. This teaching will equip you with tools to bring peace, harmony, and fun back into your marriage, as well as show you how important you are to your spouse's strength and success at home and at work.

Discover a more meaningful marriage at:
robyndykstra.com/made